THE COMPLETE GUIDE TO GAY LIFE FOR NEW EXPLORERS

The Definitive "Coming Out" Book

Michael Ryan

AuthorHouse™ UK
1663 Liberty Drive
Bloomington, IN 47403 USA
www.authorhouse.co.uk
Phone: 0800.197.4150

Published by AuthorHouse 11/22/2014

ISBN: 978-1-4969-9012-9 (sc)
ISBN: 978-1-4969-9003-7 (hc)
ISBN: 978-1-4969-9013-6 (e)

"The perfect book for helping me to accept being gay" (Steven, 16)

"Really useful stuff for finding out about gay life" (Megan 14)

"I feel so confident, happy and hopeful now" (Aaron 17)

– Quotes from Teen review group.

To my partner, Gavin.

About the Book

This book is for anyone who is unfamiliar with the gay world but has been thrown into it personally or by association and wants to know more about it.

It answers questions for people who are gay or think they might be gay and their families, friends, and supporters, including professionals such as teachers, counsellors, support workers, and doctors.

The text is written for someone of at least fourteen years of age and answers more than two hundred questions covering four main areas of gay life:

1. Questions about being gay
2. Questions asked by family and friends
3. Questions asked about the gay community, giving definitions of some common terms
4. Questions about gay sex and sexual health

Most gay people discover their sexuality in the early years of puberty and often internalise this knowledge while they come to terms with this new element of their persona.

This book aims to take the mystery out about being gay and to provide the tools for gay people (and their supporters) to accept and cope with their reality.

The content of this book is drawn from the author's professional training, his experiences, his own thoughts plus the thoughts of some of his colleagues, friends and the hundreds of teenagers and adults that he has encountered in his work.

There is nowhere else in print or online that has this amount of detail, advice and insight covering all aspects of gay life.

As this book is aimed at a wide audience, most people will dip in and out of the sections and questions that are most relevant to them. Therefore some similar answers and advice in this book have to be delivered in a number of different key areas, so apologies for any repetition if you read it cover to cover.

Acknowledgements

The completion of this book marks the end of a long process of thinking, talking, writing, rewriting, amending, editing, correcting – with lots of coffee.

Without the help of a lot of people, this book would never have happened, and I am grateful to everyone who helped me to bring the book to life.

I most want to thank my partner, Gavin Duffy, for all his guidance, advice, support, and, above all, patience.

I also want to thank my mother, Kay Ryan, who has shown to me how parents should accept their gay child – with the same openness, love, and support they give to all their children.

I want to thank those who gave me feedback on the book as it was being drafted and redrafted – Thomas McErlean, Karl Hamilton, Clodagh Ward, Esther L'Estrange, Sam L'Estrange, Mark Williamson, Steph Williamson, Gemma Dwyer, Jo O'Donoghue, Suzy Byrne, Dawn Gibson, Dean Murphy and Bernard Ryan.

Other people who helped along the journey in lots of various ways were Paul Franey, Reamonn O'Donnchadha, Sue Healy, Regan Hutchings, Breeta Geary, Ruth Duggan, Deirdre Ryan and Arlan O'Reilly.

Michael Ryan

A huge thank you to the publishers, AuthorHouse, who have baby-sat me through the process of getting this book out to the world and have been very supportive and helpful along every step of the way.

I would also especially like to thank all the teenagers and adults that I have worked with over the years who have provided the questions that I have endeavoured to answer in this book.

Contents

Questions about Being Gay

Questions from the Family of a Gay Person

Questions about the Gay Community and
Some Common Terms

Questions about Gay Sex and Sexual Health

There is a resource section at the back of this book with links to many online sites for further information and support.

Questions about Being Gay

1. What does the term *gay* mean?

Gay is a term used to describe people who are physically and romantically attracted to other people of the same gender. It can be used to describe either males or females; however, gay females are usually referred to as *lesbians* and *gay* is used mostly to refer to males.

In your early teens, you might feel attracted to people of the same gender. This may or may not mean you are gay. Some boys will see other boys as attractive, just as some girls may find other girls attractive. Perhaps this is just normal jealousy, as the other person may be better looking, fitter, smarter, wittier, more charming, or just more popular than you. Or, this attraction may just mean that you would like to be more like this person because he or she is attractive.

Being gay is a *sexual orientation*, which refers to all the various ways in which people are attracted to each other. In general terms, there are four main sexual orientations: gay, straight, asexual, and bisexual.

If you find that you are sexually attracted to a person of the same gender, that person turns you on and prompts fantasies about his or her body or sexual organs or having some sexual encounter with this person, then you are probably gay.

You may also get sexually aroused by pictures, images, or movies of people of the same gender or find that you fantasise about famous people of the same gender as you.

If so, the first thing you should do is be patient and embrace how your mind and body are developing, rather than panic or fear what you feel – which are common initial reactions for people who think they are gay. This book will answer many questions you'll have and help you to discover that it is okay to be gay – that you are perfectly normal and are equal to everyone else.

2.   What is homosexuality?

Effectively, if you are gay, you are a homosexual.

The term literally refers to an exclusive attraction to people of the same gender as you. The prefix *homo* in this context is not derived from the Latin term for *man*.

Instead, the word *homosexuality* is derived from a mix of the *homos*, meaning "same", and the Latin-derived *sexuality*, referring to the sexual element of one's life.

3.   Is being gay a choice?

No.

People do not choose to be gay. It has nothing to do with a person's upbringing, and it is not a medical issue or a psychological issue.

It is not fully known why a proportion of people in any population are gay, but it is generally accepted that between 5 and 10 per cent of all people are gay.

Animals from hundreds of species also exhibit homosexual behaviour.

4. I think I'm gay. What do I do?

Welcome to the club! You are the newest member, and you've joined up to seven hundred million other gay people around the world.

If you think you're gay, you've probably noticed that you are not attracted to people of the opposite gender, as most of your friends seem to be. You've noticed that you are instead more attracted to people of your own gender. You may be secretive about these thoughts, figuring that your thoughts are different to what others are thinking. You may also have been frightened by these thoughts and have been wondering if something is wrong with you or if you are abnormal, odd, weird, or ill.

Not to worry – these thoughts and feelings are perfectly natural. There is nothing wrong with you. You are not abnormal or odd or ill. You are just gay. This is not something that you have chosen. You may need a bit of time to accept this. You may not have thought you would be this way, and at first you may not want to accept it, but if you continue reading, you'll discover that being gay is just a part of you and not the whole of who you are.

Remember, you have done nothing wrong, you are perfectly normal, and you can be happy being gay.

5. Why am I gay?

Being gay was not something you chose, and it is just one aspect of your make-up. It is still not clear exactly why some people are gay and others are not, but nature has chosen you to be gay and it is no-one's fault – it's just nature. Most people have a "label" of some sort and yours is that you are gay. No matter what your "label" is, it is important to embrace it, but not to be defined by it. Some of the suggested theories about why homosexuality exists in nature are outlined in Q 23.

People who are born with one leg or with a disability or another feature that sets them apart from others, also ask, "Why me?"

Humans have lots of differences, and your difference is that you are gay. This does not make you inferior to straight people, just as having a birthmark or a missing limb does not make you inferior. All humans are equal and all humans have a right to live their lives in peace and to have the opportunity to make the most of their unique situation.

Being gay is only one part of you. You need to develop all parts of you and to go out there and live the best life that you can.

You are only here on this earth once, so do not let your differences get in the way of you having a great time while you are here.

6.   What is the most common age for people to realise they are gay?

The most common age at which people realise they are gay is between ten and twelve. Being so young to realise that you are attracted to people of the same gender can make life particularly confusing because before this point, you likely have been conditioned to think that boys are only attracted to girls and girls are only attracted to boys.

This realisation can also be frightening, exciting, shameful, unsettling, and even lonely if you don't feel comfortable telling anyone. You may also think it's a phase that will pass and just ignore it.

Around the age of twelve, you will probably also change to a senior school, which comes with its own pressures. You want to fit in to the new environment. You want to avoid bullies. You may need to change classes. You will likely be in a bigger school with more activity and less consistency than your old school.

At twelve, you are likely bursting to become a teenager, as this distinction comes with certain rights and privileges. It is a time of shaking off childhood habits and developing those of adulthood. These can cause preteens and teenagers untold conflicts, as they want to be treated as mini-adults but also want to be able to be childish if the mood takes them.

All these changes prove particularly difficult for gay kids, as they are dealing with so many upheavals in their lives all at the same time. They need time to adjust to the changes their bodies undergo during puberty and to deal with their new surroundings at school, new sexual desires, new ideas of adulthood, and new friends.

Parents need to be available to discuss all aspects of growing up with their children and to reassure them that if their children are gay, they as parents will be there to support them no matter what.

7.   Who can I talk to about being gay?

This is a really important question, as talking is essential for dealing with your thoughts.

It is likely that you will start developing sexual feelings in early puberty, but at approximately twelve or thirteen years old, you will start to realise which gender you have stronger feelings for.

Your schoolmates will likely talk about sex and boast about how much they know about sex and the terms related to it. As they begin experimenting, your friends will also likely boast about how much sex they are having (which is usually grossly, if not completely, exaggerated). You might hear them competing to see who gets to second base first. Boys are particularly fond of competition and exaggeration about sexual experiences.

It can be difficult to listen to your friends talk about their experiences with the opposite gender when you think you may be more interested in people of your own gender. You may join in and pretend that you fancy a particular person so that you don't feel left out, and you may also experiment with members of the opposite sex if they show interest in you.

The rest of the world may be challenging you, too. Perhaps you're also dealing with your parents' divorce, the loss of a grandparent, a medical condition, or something else – life comes with a myriad of challenges that have nothing to do with your sexuality.

Remember that around 5 to 10 per cent of all people are gay, so many other adolescents (including others in your school), are going through the same thing at the same time as you. The problem is that it can be difficult to identify them, as they may be pretending that they're not gay and may look like they know exactly what they are doing.

If you are lucky enough to be in a school where being gay is encouraged and accepted, perhaps there is a support group that you could join to help with your own situation.

If you have a close relationship with your parents and you feel they are open to discussing your thoughts about being gay, then they are perhaps the best people to broach the subject with. However, it can be difficult to open a heart-to-heart conversation with your parents, especially if these conversations aren't commonplace in your family.

On the other hand, one or both of your parents may have made it clear that they are okay with gay people, or perhaps they have gay friends. They likely will have wondered over the years whether their kids would be gay, so they are probably somewhat prepared to talk about it with you.

To begin, you may want to write them a note stating briefly that you think you might be gay or that you are gay and then let them open the conversation.

If you're sure that your family views being gay as unacceptable, you may decide to speak to an adult who isn't in your family about being gay. This could be a teacher, a relative, the school counsellor, a coach, a neighbour, or a friend's parent. If you think about the adults in your life, you might instinctively know which one is best to talk to.

If you don't feel that any adult is the right person to talk to, you may instead know of a friend who can help you through this period of questioning. Friends can be good people to talk to, but remember that they also have a lot going on in their lives and have limited life experience to draw on, so they may not be able to offer the best guidance. Also, teenagers love to have news to tell others, so be sure that the friend you hold in confidence can be trusted not to tell others about your questioning.

It is always good to have the support of someone your own age, but I would suggest that you also try to locate an adult to talk to so that you can get some balance in the advice you receive about how to deal with being gay.

If you're still struggling to decide who to discuss being gay with, you can join one of the many Internet forums, chat rooms, and websites available to teenagers that can offer great support and guidance from people going through situations similar to yours – like www.itgetsbetter.org

The Internet can offer you good advice, support, networking, and a safe place for you to discuss your sexuality, but beware – Internet forums provide little screening of what is put up for discussion, and homophobes may log on and write nasty stuff which you have to rise above.

In some of the larger cities there are often youth groups within LGBT organizations for supporting gay adolescents. If you do decide to try this type of support you might bring someone you trust to come along with you to your first meeting or ask the organizers to meet you at the venue to let you know what you can expect.

Many countries also have hotlines that people who wish to discuss their sexuality can call, and your country may even have lines specifically for gay, bisexual, lesbian, and transgender people to call. An Internet search will help you find the closest one to you – *See Resources section at back of book.*

These lines are often answered by professionally qualified volunteers, and they may be of the same sexual orientation as you and have been through what you're going through. Many of these people volunteer because they didn't have access to such a service when they were growing up and they want to be sure that you have someone to talk to whom you can trust.

8.   If I am gay, will I bring shame to my family?

No.

Shame is a perception, not an actual event or object. Some families have strong views about what is right and wrong for their members, and all families have moral codes and values that determine what is acceptable and what is shameful. For example, your family might view lying, stealing, cheating, or failure as shameful and see any family member who chooses to engage in these activities as bringing shame on the family name.

But remember that being gay is not a choice – it is merely a fact of life. It is not something that you have control over. If your family script says it is shameful to be gay, then the script is flawed.

Some families view mental disorders as shameful, as if a family member suffering from such a disorder set out to be depressed, schizophrenic, or psychotic. This view may cause them to ostracise the suffering person, when they really need all the support and love that they can get. This again is a flaw.

Families may similarly decide that not being clever or not being good at sports or being left-handed or being disfigured somehow goes against the family ethos. Again, this is a dysfunction in the family script and unfair to the family member who is different.

Do not buy into the shame if your family try to impose it on you for being gay. You have done nothing wrong. However, you may wish to help your family rethink their values.

9.   If I tell my parents I'm gay, what will happen?

Parents' reactions vary greatly depending on their personal views of homosexuality, their standing within the community, the culture you are brought up in, their place in their religious community, their place in business, their public image, their age, and their previous experiences with gay people.

Some parents will hug their kids and say they still love them (as mine did). Others will be shocked or overcome with fear, confusion, or other emotions. Still others will deny what you have just told them or will try to ignore it.

In all cases, parents need time to digest what they have been told and to adjust to the idea that their child is gay. Your parents might be consumed by the idea that you may not provide grandchildren for them and will need time to mourn the potential loss.

They may also have learned incorrect information about AIDS and other sexually transmitted infections (STIs). They may have to reconcile your sexuality with their religious beliefs. They may incorrectly believe that being gay is all about sex. They may need reassurance that you are still the same child they know and love and that being gay does not need to change anything between you.

They may ask loads of questions and they may need to read this book or other material from gay-related supports and websites to understand the various aspects of what life is like for a gay person.

In the most extreme situations, parents who are not able to deal with the news may ask the child to leave the home while they consider it – See Question 16.

It is most likely that your parents will not alter your living situation. Instead, they will just need time to come around. As with any change a family experiences, family members will likely experience a period of coolness as everyone adjusts to the new-normal. After that, the family will carry on with everyday life.

You will know when your parents are becoming comfortable with the news. This might happen when they start make light-hearted comments about it or when they once again take an active interest in your social life.

10.   How do I tell my parents that I'm gay?

This can be a very straightforward process or a tricky one. Over the years, you will have gathered whether your parents are comfortable with gay people. Many parents already have an inkling when one of their children is gay before he or she tells them.

If you are closer to one parent, perhaps this is the person to tell first. If you have an equal relationship with both, perhaps have the conversation when you can sit with them alone and without any distractions or interruptions.

If you can't guarantee such private time at your home, you may need to ask your parents for a private word and arrange a suitable time and place for the discussion.

When the time arrives, you'll probably experience a moment of tension, and you may find it difficult to say the words "I am gay" or "I think I am gay."

Take your time. You may cry, you may laugh nervously, and you may feel butterflies in your tummy, but you need to say the words. You may decide to write them down and pass the note to your parents and even ask them to read it when you've left the room. You might just come straight out and say, "I am gay," and see what happens. Your parents might be prepared for this news, but they may also be shocked by it.

When you tell them, allow a little time for the news to sink in. They are likely to be flooded with thoughts and may say something like the following:

• You may never give us grandkids?

- How will I tell the neighbours or family?

- This is against our beliefs!

- How can we fix this?

- This is just a phase!

- How could this happen?

- Have I done something wrong?

- Who else might be gay and isn't telling me?

- What do I do?

- How can I accept this?

- What will people think?

- How could you do this to us?

- How long have you known?

- Why did you not tell us before?

- What do we do now?

You may not have all the answers to their questions, and that's okay. Give them this book.

Throughout the talk, they may be happy, angry, confused, unsure, stuck for words, panicky, upset, and maybe even indifferent.

Most parents realise that there is a chance their kids will be gay, and your parents may even have anticipated this scene happening at some point. No matter what, they will need time to adjust and seek advice and support, perhaps from other parents who have been through this scenario.

You'll likely find that your parents will adjust to the situation and will completely accept you when they know that you're gay. They're still your parents and they brought you into the world, so they'll want to have you around as long as they are alive.

Once they accept that you have not chosen to be gay and that this is just one element of being human, they will realise that no one has done anything wrong and that they just need to get on with their normal lives – just as you want to get on with your normal life.

Try to avoid coming out first on a social networking site. If you do, your parents will probably hear the news second or third hand, and it will be difficult for you to contain who the news spreads to and how your friends and family report it to each other.

When parents hear such a disclosure from a third party, they may believe that they weren't available to you when you were going through a period of confusion or loneliness, and they may feel inadequate. So, it is important that they learn that you are gay directly from you.

11.   When will my parents accept that I'm gay?

This ranges from immediately to never.

Your parents may have grown up in a time or place where their religious community's or neighbours' views of them were of the utmost importance, and they may have been taught to think of homosexuality as something negative.

Over time, the developed world has come to accept that gay people are human beings with all the same emotions, feelings, and desires as everyone else and that the fact that they are attracted to people of their own gender is not something they chose or sought out.

Your parents will have been exposed to more openly gay people in the past ten years than ever before as more and more public figures have declared that they are gay. At last, the general public can put faces and names to the gay world that was hidden from them for so long.

Now everyone can see that gay people come from every walk of life and that most are decent, clever, creative, educated, skilled, talented, and ambitious in addition to being non-threatening, ordinary, everyday people going about their business.

In time, most parents come to accept the fact that their sons or daughters are gay, and they want these children to be happy, as they want all their children to be happy.

However, some parents can't change the views their cultural, religious, or social groups have instilled in them, and they reject their gay children in order to save face in their communities. This is such a shame, as they miss out on their children's development and will never be able to share in the relationships, successes, and achievements their children have along the way.

Gay friends can fill the gaps left by unaccepting family members by supporting each other through tough times as they carry on with their normal lives.

12. My parents think being gay is just a phase and that I'll grow out of it. How can I convince them that this is permanent?

You have known for some time that you're gay, and you've had time to get used to this fact, but your parents may be having their first experience with the gay world. They will naturally want you to be happy, but they may also have a lot of concerns, fears, and worries about your being gay.

It may take them time to accept that you're gay. In the meantime, they may hope that your feelings for people of the same gender will pass as your hormones settle down.

During this time, you will need to be patient with them. As you explain what life is like for you over time, they will gradually realise that you are not going through a phase and that you actually are gay.

Give them time and this book. Parents usually come around.

13. Someone else outed the fact that I'm gay. What do I do when my parents ask about it?

When you realise that someone has broken your confidence, even if they thought they were doing the right thing by informing your parents that they know you're gay, the first thing you are likely to do is fly into a blind panic.

You may initially default to the usual teenage strategy of lying to your parents in order to get out of trouble and regain control. You may even contemplate harming yourself. Neither of these are the answer. If you really feel like harming yourself, seek out a trusted adult to talk to, and keep yourself safe. It's not unusual to feel this way, but it is really important that you do not act on these feelings.

The fear you feel inside you is fear of the unknown, and this could cause you to jump to the worst possible conclusion. Remember, though, that what happens next might not be difficult at all.

The best thing to do is to face the situation head-on and go straight to your parents. Whatever is going to happen will happen.

Prepare yourself for this conversation by telling yourself that you have done nothing wrong and that you are not responsible for being gay but that you are responsible for living your life, and your parents need to support you on that journey.

They may be defensive when you speak to them, or they may be calm. They may feel hurt having heard it from someone else and will wonder why you didn't tell them directly.

Try to remain calm and discuss what they have heard in a mature way. Let them know that you are not ashamed of being gay, and remind them that the fact that you are gay is not a problem that has to be solved but a reality that has to be adjusted to.

If someone caught you experimenting with someone else and so told your parents, that person and your parents should realise that that this is a normal part of every adolescent's development. Your parents may need time to adjust to the fact that you are growing up – regardless of your sexual orientation.

Your parents may have fears about you being bullied and harassed at school, and they'll likely have concerns about your safety and your future. That's their job.

You may need to explain that this is all new to you also and that you are still trying to figure out what is happening to you and that you, too, need time to adjust to the fact that you are gay. Your parents might find that this is a good time to inform you about safe sex, and they'll probably encourage you to wait to have sex till you're older. Ultimately, your parents just want what's best for you.

If you have declared your sexual orientation to someone, who then spread the word without your permission, it can be difficult to manage the reactions of those you didn't choose to tell. It can be more challenging if everyone knows that you are gay before you've had time to prepare yourself for being "this week's talking point" among your peers. You need to keep your supporters close at this time. They can help you get through this difficult period.

Being outed without your consent is a breach of trust, so and you'll need to be cautious about how you disclose other information to that person who outed you.

Being outed can also get the message out there that you are gay and if it you're outed, you should stand tall and accept the fact that everyone knows. To try and deny that the disclosure is true is probably fruitless, as people will have made up their minds about it anyway, and you'll only exhaust yourself if you try to contain the rumour-mill. To deny it can also indicate to others that you are ashamed of being gay, but you have nothing to be ashamed about.

Just accept that this is not an ideal situation for you, but remember that it's not a catastrophe. Keep your dignity in the fact that you're gay and proud to be so.

14. I told my parents that I'm gay, and they dismissed it and haven't brought it up since. What do I do?

This situation happens less frequently now than in the past, but unfortunately, it still happens, and you will need to learn how to manage it. Your parents may be conservative or in denial because they cannot accept the fact that they have a gay child. This can be a difficult situation for you because this is something central to your character.

Your parents grew up in a different era, so they may not have ever had to deal with the issue of homosexuality before. They may have strong religious beliefs and may wish to remain faithful to them, and ignoring the fact that you're gay may be a way for them to avoid amending their religious or moral stance on the issue.

They may also have had negative experiences with homosexuals that have left them with sour memories. Perhaps a gay person made an advance on one of your parents in their youth, leaving them to view homosexuals as predators.

If you wish to challenge such long-held views, you can bring up the topic from time to time, remind them that being gay is something that you do not have control over, and demonstrate that you are different from the negative stereotypes or people that they have met in the past. Your parents may seem to be the bearers of all knowledge, but sometimes children must educate their parents about today's world.

If they continue to ignore the fact that you're gay, you may decide to seek support about your sexuality outside the family. If you find that their views are unmovable, rather than risk damaging your relationship, you may choose to leave this element of your life out of family discussions.

You do not need your parents to be fully onboard, as you can get the support for this part of your life elsewhere. Sometimes the fight is not worth it.

15.   Will I be rejected if I come out as being gay?

You will never be rejected by the gay community for being gay.

Some people's families, religious communities, or cultures have not yet accepted that being gay is simply a part of life. As you grow up within these groups, you'll become aware whether other group members will accept your being gay.

However, it is not always possible to accurately predict what others will do if you come out. Most families love their children regardless of their sexual orientation, but your parents could have an extreme reaction and choose to follow the dogma of their religion or culture, and they may not understand that being gay is not a choice.

If you encounter such an extreme response, you may find that it is better to seek out other members of the gay community for support and understanding around your sexual orientation.

You can always turn to your family or other social groups for additional support around other aspects of your life.

Gay people are being accepted as equals more and more widely, but some cultures are quicker to adopt that mindset than others.

You deserve to live a happy life even while you wait for some societies to catch up.

16.   What do I do if my parents throw me out when I tell them that I'm gay?

Fewer and fewer people are excluded from their families as time goes on, but some parents are still staunchly homophobic. If you do get thrown out, are not yet a legal adult, and have nowhere to go, you can go to the police and inform them of your situation. They will contact government social services, who will ensure that you have somewhere to stay.

This is a last resort, though. You should first try to see if a trusted neighbour, friend, or relative will take you in until they have a chance to speak with your parents.

This trusted adult may be able to help your parents accept what they have learned about you and realise that they over-reacted and that they just need time to adjust.

I need to emphasise that being thrown out of the family home is an extreme reaction and that it happens very seldom, but it can happen. If it does, focus on the people who do support you, and perhaps in time, your parents will realise that being gay is not something you have chosen and will welcome you back.

17.   What will my brothers and sisters say when they find out that I'm gay?

If you're comfortable telling your siblings that you're gay, you're entitled to their respect. Because your brothers and sisters have also grown up in a time when gay people are in TV shows, movies, and bands and are famous members of the fashion, entertainment, business, and political realms, it is most likely that they will be fine with your being gay.

However, some siblings feel awkward about having a gay brother/sister, as they fear others may think that they, too, are gay or that there is a gay gene in the family. They usually need a little time to stop focussing on themselves before they come around to accepting the fact that you're gay. Afterwards, they might even stand up for you if you're bulled or harassed.

Of course, some siblings don't accept their gay siblings, particularly if their parents are homophobic, or they may ignore the fact or deny it if they're confronted, just as some parents do. In this circumstance, you can only reassure them that you're still the same brother or sister that you were before you came out and that you still love them.

Bear in mind that one of your siblings may also be gay and not yet have dealt with it themselves. Your announcement may put pressure on them as they cope with their own identity.

18. How long will it take people besides my parents to accept that I'm gay?

From a second to a lifetime. Some people will already know you're gay before you tell them and will have already accepted it. Others may have long-held beliefs about gay people that need to be adjusted in their own minds before they can accept it, and this can take some time.

As being gay was not your choice, you have nothing to apologise for. You may need to give some people longer to accept that you're gay than others, but most will eventually come around. That said, if some people refuse to accept you as a full and worthwhile human being, then you might be better off not having these people in your life.

Because your grandparents are from an earlier generation, they may not be able to comprehend what being gay is. You may decide that telling them is not worth the worry that it will bring to them.

On the other hand, I have often been surprised at who is tolerant and who is closed-minded. You, too, might be surprised who supports you and who reacts very differently from what you anticipated.

19.   Is there something wrong with me because I'm gay?

Absolutely not.

Being gay is just as common as being left-handed, and like a left-hander, you are perfectly normal and equal to everyone else.

People who discover they are gay often feel like there is something wrong, like they are abnormal, or like they have a big malfunction, and they sometimes want to ignore it and hope it goes away.

Adjusting to being gay can be a really difficult, lonely, confusing, and isolating time, even though you may be surrounded by people, friends, family, and classmates. You may try to act as if everything is okay, yet you have to deal with all these strange feelings and desires. You may feel that you can't confide in anyone because you don't know what to say. You may feel like it's wrong to be attracted to someone of the same gender as yourself, but you will also likely realise that no matter what you do, you cannot stop these feelings.

Realise that being gay is just the orientation that nature has chosen for you. It's not wrong, it's nothing to feel ashamed about, it's not unnatural, and there's nothing you need to do to change it or to become anyone else. Celebrate the fact that you're gay and that this is just one part of you being a good and worthwhile person.

20.   If I'm gay, does that mean I hate people of the opposite gender?

No.

In fact, many gay males get on better with females than straight males, and many lesbians have many male friends. Being gay has nothing to do with hate or anger. It is only to do with sexual orientation, with being attracted to the same gender as yourself.

21.   Is being gay normal?

Yes.

Every person who finds him or herself in a small group with some sort of difference from others in mainstream society feels somewhat marginalised, but it's these differences that make the human race as interesting as it is.

Being gay is normal. It is a significant part of your identity and it is important that you embrace being gay, and do not view yourself in any negative way because of it.

No two humans are alike, and it is our differences that make us unique. Being gay certainly puts you in a minority group within society, but so does being a genius or being really tall, and these traits don't make the people who have them abnormal.

If you choose to go against your nature, you choose a life-long struggle. Accept and love yourself, and others will too!

22.   Is being gay natural?

Yes.

Nature has created people with unique qualities, including being gay, and because gay people are part of nature, it is natural to be gay.

In the womb, all foetuses start out as female forms, and around week six, a foetus with the male Y chromosome will develop testes, which produce the male hormone testosterone. Around week eight, the testosterone is released and masculinises the body and the brain. The brain needs to absorb a certain amount of testosterone to pre-dispose the male to be attracted to females. If the brain absorbs less testosterone, then the male is more likely to grow up to be gay or bisexual.

If foetuses with two X chromosomes are exposed to higher than average levels of the hormone androgen as they develop in the womb, this can result in them being more attracted to females.

Neither of these explanations are definitive, as researchers do not yet fully understand the exact reasons why some people are attracted to their same gender.

Humans are only one of a myriad of life forms on earth, and homosexuality has been observed in around 1,500 species of animals, so gay people are not that special, even within the whole of the animal kingdom.

23.   Why has nature made some people gay?

There is no definitive answer to this question, but nature has a way of finding purposeful lives for everyone, and everyone has a role within society.

One theory is that nature has created a certain proportion of the population to be homosexual, and because these people generally do not have children, this leaves a pool of people without young to look after, available to react to crises.

This manifests other benefits, too. When elderly people require additional care, a gay son or daughter is more likely to be available than his or her siblings who themselves may be trying to rear a family. If an elderly person has an accident and requires immediate attention, it is more likely for gay children than their siblings to be able to drop everything to get their elderly relative into care.

They may also be available to assist their other family members when, say, a child is ill or has an emergency and the parent needs someone they can trust to mind their flock temporarily while they tend to the sick child.

During a global emergency, gay people may also be more readily available to mobilise to assist others, as they do not always have to concern themselves with their own children's welfare before moving to action.

Gay people may also be available to adopt and foster children when parents die or are not capable of looking after their young.

Some people suggest that homosexuality is a way of keeping the population of the world from getting too high, as gay people will not produce as many children as if they were straight.

All cultures require a certain number within their ranks to be unburdened by childrearing to create, invent, care for others, philosophise, entertain, travel, observe, and think. A large proportion of the world's greatest inventors, artists, thinkers, and philosophers were and are gay!

Of course, many heterosexual people do all these things too, but they may need to rearrange more stuff in their lives in order to do them.

24. Can a traumatic event cause someone to become gay?

No.

Traumatic events hurt anyone involved in them, but no study has proved that any event, even sexual abuse, can cause people to change their sexual orientation.

Some people who have been abused might be confused about their sexuality as they mature. It is important that they receive appropriate counselling and support from qualified therapists to ensure that the abused person can appropriately develop mentally, sexually and physically.

25. Can being gay be just a phase?

No.

Being gay cannot be a phase. However, when normally curious teenagers explore their own sexuality, they will sometimes experiment with same-sex activity. This can be exciting and fun and is generally harmless. Many teens play out the "show me yours and I'll show you mine" routine, and some touching or fondling among consenting teens is not unusual.

At this stage, teenagers may think that they are gay because they have engaged in and even enjoyed such an activity with others of the same gender, but this does not necessarily mean they are gay. Consistent sexual urges and persistent attraction to people of the same gender are required for someone to be gay.

Thus, a one-off curious incident does not make someone gay. That said, straight teenagers may inform their parents that they are gay afterwards to shock or annoy them.

If you are gay, help your parents understand that this is something you have thought about for some time and that you are at least fairly sure that you are instinctually more attracted to people of your own gender.

26. Are gay people just confused?

No.

Once gay people pass through puberty, they will not be confused about their sexuality. They will know exactly who they are attracted to.

The confusion usually occurs in the early teens, when people are expected to be attracted to, date, and prepare to settle down with someone of the opposite gender. As they progress through puberty, they realise that this traditional idea of relationships does not feel comfortable and that they are attracted to people of their own gender. Although they secretly know who they really fancy, they will usually try to conform to their peers and date opposite-gender partners. To the outside world, they present an image that everything is going according to the traditional plan, so when they come out as being gay, their friends and family members may be confused.

Each person is entitled to explore his or her own path of discovery, and that may mean experimenting with relationships with the opposite gender and with the same gender. Each person will eventually settle into what feels natural for them.

If you are truly gay, be careful not to let your experiments with the opposite gender go so far that you find yourself getting married to someone who is unaware that you are gay. This is unfair to your partner, your potential family, and yourself.

27.   How do I know whether I'm gay or not?

During puberty, your body goes through changes which are well documented in biology books. As these take place, you'll also notice for the first time that you seek affection and love outside of the family home. This marks the beginning of your process of seeking a partner with whom to establish your own relationship into the future.

Most people are straight, so those around you will assume that you'll choose a partner of the opposite gender, and most of your friends and peers will discuss flirting and romances from a straight perspective.

If you find that you're not as easily distracted by the opposite gender as your own and that your feelings are directed towards people of your own gender more than towards the opposite gender, these may be the first indications that you're gay.

As you go through puberty, you may find that you have sexual thoughts only about people of the same gender, and you may find that some of your mannerisms are slightly different to those stereotypical for straight people.

If you're unsure of the way society will treat you as a gay person, you may decide to camouflage your true feelings for the sake of conformity and decide to date people of the opposite gender. You'll probably also feel that it's worth a shot if you're not sure if you're straight or gay till you try it.

If dating the opposite gender does not go according to plan or you just don't feel it, it's likely that you'll be unable to shake your attraction to the same gender. At this point, it's likely that you might be gay, and it's best to work towards becoming comfortable with the idea.

During these teenage years, you'll also have all kinds of questions about yourself – am I into rock or pop?, am I grumpy or happy?, sloppy or neat?, square or cool? Asking whether you're gay or straight or somewhere in between is just one of these.

You'll need some time to consider your questions about your sexuality. Some people are lucky and know straight away whether they're straight or gay, but not everyone does. Many people need to let their hormones settle down before they can be sure, with some people getting into their twenties, thirties, or even later to understand exactly what their sexual orientation is.

If you find that you're exclusively attracted to people of your own gender and you only get sexually aroused by thoughts of kissing, caressing, and fondling people of the same gender as yourself, then you probably are gay. If you have the same feelings about girls and boys, you may be bisexual, and if you only fantasise about and get aroused by members of the opposite gender, you are probably straight (heterosexual).

It's important to trust your arousal messages, but having an attraction to people of your own gender does not absolutely mean that you are gay. It may simply mean that you're envious of the physical development, intelligence, skills, or physical appearance of members of your gender. But if you find that they sexually arouse you, then you are probably gay.

Try not to obsess about whether you're gay or straight once these feelings begin. Let them happen. Enjoy observing the way your mind and body react to the different genders. In time it will become clear which way you consistently sway, and then you can go about accepting your orientation.

28.   I think I'm gay. How can I be sure?

During your teenage years and early adulthood, you'll notice that you're naturally aroused by a particular gender. Most people are turned on by the opposite gender, but some people are only turned on by people of their own gender, and others, bisexuals, are turned on by both genders.

All people's orientations fall somewhere on a continuum from exclusively gay to exclusively straight, with perfect bisexuality right in the middle. Few people are actually exclusive in their orientation and most people will have some element of bisexual thoughts or urges throughout their lifetime. Where you fall on this continuum will become clear when you allow your mind the freedom to follow its natural attractions.

When you first feel attracted to people of your own gender, you may resist your feelings and try to be attracted to people of the opposite gender. However, if these attempts do not feel natural to you, you'll become frustrated. Remember that your sexual orientation is not something you choose – it chooses you.

Allow yourself to feel whatever you feel, be turned on by whoever turns you on, fantasise about whatever you naturally fantasise, and safely experiment with whatever feels right. As you do so, you may find that you're persistently turned on by people of your own gender. Then, it's likely that you're gay. Welcome to the club! Sit back, relax, and enjoy.

Being gay is not like a career. It's not something you do some of the time, not something you practise, not something you can give up, and not something that comes and goes. Being gay is at the core of your existence; it is part of your make-up.

To put it another way, if you're consistently and exclusively attracted to people of the same gender as you, then you're gay. If you dream of sexual activities with people of the same gender or use images of people of the same gender for arousal, then you're gay. If you enjoy sex only with someone of the same gender, then you're gay. However, if you have fleeting thoughts about what it might like to have sex with someone of your own gender but get turned on only by people of the opposite gender, then you're probably straight.

Sex is often a taboo topic that many people are left to deal with alone. But sexual urges and sexual orientation are a natural part of who you are and should be discussed in the same way as you would discuss other changes such as growing tall, developing muscles, and developing psychologically. I recommend that you find an adult whom you trust to discuss how you feel about your sexuality as a natural part of your development. Adults were once teenagers, so they know how confusing, awkward, and challenging it is to negotiate sexual development.

I also recommend that you not try to deal with confusion about your sexual orientation alone. It's difficult to know exactly what's going on, as sexual feelings are all new to you. Rest assured you are not the only one in your year, your grade, your community, or your neighbourhood who is dealing with being gay. You may not even be the only one in your family who is dealing with challenges around their sexual orientation.

Youth support groups have sprung up in many parts of the world to help younger people deal with their sexuality. You may find it helpful to join such a group so that you can meet others in the same boat as you. *See links in resources section to find a group.*

29.   Can I choose not to be gay?

You cannot choose your sexual orientation, but you can choose to control how you behave in response to your sexuality, as with any sexual orientation.

You may decide not to take part in gay sexual activity and to remain celibate (to not have sex with others). You can also choose to pretend to be heterosexual and live life accordingly, but to do so would be to deny a perfectly normal aspect of yourself. This would also deny any straight partner that you choose to settle down with, the chance for them to meet someone who is truly attracted to him or her physically, sexually and emotionally.

Such situations can leave partners without the chance to truly fulfil their lives. The children that these unions produce have to deal with the fallout of broken relationships if the gay adults later decide to be true to themselves. The thing is, nature has made you gay, and to live the happiest life possible, you need to be true to your nature.

Some therapists say they can reverse people's sexuality. They often attempt this with neuro-linguistic programming, which is a loose form of hypnotherapy. This programming merely alters subjects' thinking about homosexuality but does not affect their true sexuality, and their homosexual desires eventually re-emerge.

Gay people often fear coming out because they may be ostracised by their families, their communities, and even their countries. Being gay can be very difficult if the people around you make damning statements and violent threats against gay people, and hearing these can make you fear the worst for yourself.

But take heart. No one is forcing you to come out if you feel it's unsafe to expose the fact that you're gay. Instead, you can choose to remove yourself from such an environment when you're legally an adult so you can attend support groups to help you cope with your sexuality or live in a more liberal area where you can be yourself.

You may initially hate the fact that you're gay, and that feeling would be natural, but you won't always feel like that. Once you can explore the gay scene and make friends with those who accept gay people for who they are, you'll learn to accept being gay, and life won't seem as hard as it does now.

You cannot change being gay. You can't opt out of it. It's just the way nature has made you. This may seem harsh and cold, but that's the way it is. You have only one life to live, so you need to find a way to make the most of the skills, opportunities, and challenges that have been handed to you.

All too often, gay teenagers feel that they will never be able to accept that they're gay and complete suicide before they ever really give living a chance. *Problems are temporary – suicide is permanent.* Even if life seems too difficult now, take heart that it will get easier once you have the freedom to choose your life. You will choose a fabulous life.

You have to stay alive to fulfil your desires and make your dreams come true, so choose life!

Hundreds of millions of other gay people around the world are all trying to figure out how to live authentic lives and still be happy, just like you are.

Give yourself some credit for having the smarts to get through difficult times and for having the bravery to face your challenges. You didn't choose to be gay, but you are. Learn to love yourself for being you. No one else on earth has your exact set of circumstances, and you need to love all of you, including the gay part, and live life to the fullest.

I must emphasise that *problems are temporary but suicide is permanent.* If you chose suicide, there's no turning back, and you'll never know how successful you would have been. You will likely find that only during adolescence does being gay seem like a problem. After that, it becomes a part of who you are, and you can accept it and live your life. If you ever contemplate suicide or self harm, you must say this to a trusted adult or tell your Doctor. If you can't find either, you should go to the emergency department at your local hospital and tell them how you are feeling. They will provide immediate services to keep you safe.

Hating being gay only leads to bitterness, and let's face it, no one wants to be bitter all the time. So choose to accept who you are. You'll free yourself from hatred and bitterness, and you'll discover that you can have a great life as a gay person.

30.   How do I accept that I'm gay?

Rather than viewing being gay as something you have to accept, you can choose to view it as something to celebrate. *Accepting* that you're gay makes it sound like something you have to endure or conquer or something that has defeated you. This is an unhealthy way to look at the situation. You are gay, and you will be gay for the rest of your life – just as you'll have eyes of the same colour for the rest of your life. You can choose to wear coloured contact lenses, but underneath, your eyes are still the same colour.

Instead, it's healthy to celebrate the character traits that life has given you, and endeavour to incorporate these traits into the best life you can have.

Accepting that you're gay is liberating. Before this happens, you may avoid dealing with it, wish it away, try to be straight, reject your feelings and desires, and see yourself as odd. But once you accept that you're gay, the pressure of denial will be released, and you'll feel a huge sense of relief, and can be happy with yourself. Then you can focus on helping your friends and family to catch up and accept you too.

31.   How long will it take me to become comfortable with being gay?

That depends on where you start. If you have internalised homophobic messages from those around you (*see* Question 128), it may be useful to discuss these messages with a counsellor, therapist, or gay support group.

Once you accept that you've done nothing wrong, that you're a good and worthwhile person, that you're entitled to be happy, you can then accept the way nature has made you. You're reading this book, so you're almost there.

You get to decide how much you wish other people to know about your sexuality, based on how you believe those in your culture, family, society, workplace, and religion will react to the information.

To not accept yourself as being gay will likely prolong the hurt you feel and could leave your life feeling unfulfilled. It is easiest to accept that you're gay and to choose to live a great life. Remember, too, that being gay is just one part of you. Here on earth, there are so many things to do, see, achieve, and experience that have nothing to do with your sexuality.

32.   At what age do most people come out as being gay?

Some children declare their sexuality as young as age five if they are aware of it and if they feel comfortable telling others about it.

That said, according to an EU based survey, the average age that people tell others they're gay is seventeen (this age is slightly older in the U.S. - between eighteen and twenty one).

If we consider that the average age people discover they're gay is between ten and twelve and the average age they disclose this to others is approx. seventeen, then we see that most gay people go through at least a five-year period of dealing with their sexuality on their own, which can be a lonely and tough thing to do.

Most gay teenagers find it difficult to tell anyone about their sexuality, but as time goes on, the average age of disclosure is getting younger, so that period of loneliness and living with a secret is getting shorter.

33.   When should I come out?

When you're ready.

You'll realise at some point that you're not just going through a phase, and your mind will settle with the idea that you'll remain gay. The sooner you realise this and are able to tell this to others, the less lonely dealing with your sexuality will be for you.

Some people tell others that they're gay as soon as they realise that their sexual orientation is different to their friends. Some gay people just wait until they feel comfortable to tell others about it. Some people wait until they're caught doing something that exposes the fact that they're gay, and some people never tell anyone.

The last option can make life difficult. People who choose this constantly need to watch their backs to ensure people don't pick up on something they say or do that might expose them. Many such people live lonely lives without partners, or even marry someone of the opposite gender just to keep other people from guessing that they're gay. Those who do marry the opposite gender create difficult situations for themselves, their spouse and their kids, as these relationships are seldom built on mutual romantic love.

34.   How do I come out of the closet?

There are many and varied ways for you to come out. Below are a few suggestions and you'll figure out the best way for you.

Some people choose to first tell a friend or a trusted adult outside their immediate families such as a teacher, counsellor, aunt or uncle, or coach. If you talk to such a trusted adult, they will likely offer you support so you can explore how others will receive your news, and you may find that the people you tell aren't surprised. As you choose who to tell first, be careful to select someone you believe will keep your conversation confidential until you're ready to tell others.

Some people are comfortable telling their parents first. Or they may decide to tell one parent first and then seek advice about how to tell the other parent.

You may also decide to tell a friend or family member who is around your age.

Whomever you tell, be prepared to answer a lot of questions, and also be prepared in case that person turns out to be less supportive than you imagined.

Most people will receive the news well and won't mind. Others may need time to digest the news and then come back to you with questions.

Coming out on a social media site first, may not be the best way of letting the world knows that you're gay, as people close to you may feel offended that you didn't trust them enough to approach them personally. Posting this news on these sites also leaves you open to abusive remarks, as your peers might not be expecting the news, and you may have to answer a lot of questions and comments that you hadn't prepared for.

35.   Who should I come out to first?

A person you can trust to keep your confidence.

If you feel ready to tell someone you're gay, you've probably been dealing the idea for a long time and will have realised that you're not just going through a phase. At that point, you might decide to tell your best friend in the hope that he or she will support you, while you decide who else to tell. You might decide that your parents or one parent should know first and that together you can tell others when the time is right. Or you could tell a teacher or the school counsellor if you have a good relationship with that person.

You should choose a person whom you trust to keep the news to him or herself, as you have the right to control who knows, and when. It's also helpful to choose someone who can support you as you tell others.

The sooner you tell someone, the less time you'll be alone in dealing with being gay.

36.   Do gay people lose friends when they come out?

Sometimes, but that happens less often now than it did in the past.

Friends often know when their pals are gay before they come out. That said, the news could be a big shock, particularly to really close friends.

Your best friend may find the news difficult to hear. A friend might fear that everyone will now question if they, too, are gay and initially reject you to ensure everyone else knows that they are still straight (and possibly available) and not into this gay stuff. However, such friends usually come around eventually, and although the relationship may be different, it will usually continue. The friendship might even be stronger because of this new trust in each other.

Many straight teens find it cool to have a gay friend because it shows that they're up to speed with social norms, that they're comfortable in their own sexuality, and it shows that they can accept everyone in society.

37.   Am I inferior if I'm gay?

Absolutely not. Gay people are equal to everyone else in every respect. You are a great human being.

Saying that gay people are inferior, is tantamount to saying those with a particular skin colour are inferior to others. We have seen how this type of thinking has affected black people – they have had to struggle to ensure they are seen as equal, just as gay people have.

Historically, humans stigmatised anything that made people different from the majority out of fear, superstition, and ignorance.

As the human race has developed, we've come to realise that everyone is equal and that our individual differences benefit society. People who still see those with differences as inferior have not reached your level of development or your level of maturity.

If you deal with your sexuality in a healthy manner, you will develop appropriately.

38.   Is being gay wrong?

No.

Being gay is just how nature has designed you. As you have not chosen to be gay, it cannot be wrong. You can have a full life as an active participant in your society, community, and culture.

People who say that being gay is wrong just do not know how life works. However, it is difficult to deny that you're gay, or to try to be someone you're not. Being true to yourself will keep you free from the shackles of a false existence.

39.   Does being gay define my life?

No.

Being gay is just one facet of someone's life. It is a part of their make-up that permeates all aspects of their existence, but sexuality alone is not something that defines a person. Unlike all other species of mammals, humans have unique ways to think, experience, sympathise, empathise, logicise, philosophise, imagine, create, invent and observe - and how you take part in all of these activities makes you who you are.

Being gay means that you are attracted to someone of your own gender, but this should not monopolise your thoughts, actions, and opinions.

40.   Should I experiment sexually in order to know whether I'm gay or not?

Before you choose to experiment, remember that any such activities should occur only between people who are both consenting and within the laws of your country and with respect to the boundaries of your families' teachings. You can check the age of consent in your country by going to this website - www.avert.org/age-sexual-consent.htm

Remember, too, that sexual contact carries risks, and you need to protect yourself from sexually transmitted infections (STIs) and from pregnancy (if you experiment with the opposite gender). More information about safe sex appears later in the book.

As you go through your teenage years, you may connect with other people who are also curious about whether they're gay. At first, you may avoid each other, as you may not want others to know that you may have this quality in common. You may even become arch-enemies to show the world that you're not gay or to convince others that you disapprove of anything or anyone that's gay.

But when you become more comfortable with yourself and as your hormones tell you more persistently that you fancy people of the same gender, you may decide to seek out someone to experiment with. This can be a difficult time, particularly if neither of you are out. As a result, you might engage in a game of innuendo and flirtation to test whether you're both "on the same bus". As this goes on, you may orchestrate a way for you to be alone with this other person, and then it's up to one of you to make a physical gesture to show that you find the other person attractive. If the move is accepted, then you'll likely engage in some form of sexual exploration together. This could involve caressing, kissing, or fondling. This is probably enough at first to assure yourselves that you're on the right track. This may be a first for both of you and could be quite special, quite clumsy, quite exciting, quite disappointing and probably quite messy.

First encounters rarely lead to meaningful relationships, although that's not unheard of, but no matter what the outcome is, it is healthy to remain friendly afterwards, as you probably live close to the person you experiment with and are going through the same thing at the same time.

You have a responsibility for keeping the information about the other person's sexuality confidential, as he or she may not be out and may need time, just as you do, to take in all that has happened. It is not your business to out anyone.

It's probably healthiest to choose partners close to your own age to begin with. When you're older, you can choose partners from a wider range of ages.

People your own age may not be as advanced as you or may be more developed than you. Sexual maturity is not a race, and everyone will develop at a pace that is natural for them.

If you are experimenting with someone older or younger than you, learn about your local laws concerning the age of consent for people having sex and be sure that what you're doing is legal.

Be wary of people who are much older than you. They may seem experienced and knowledgeable about all things gay, but you need to ensure that they will not try to take advantage of you.

Prepubescent children (not yet teenagers) are *never* part of this process. It is imperative that you *do not* engage sexually in any way with children. Apart from it being immoral and illegal, doing so would damage a child's natural development and could result in psychological trauma for the child. Prepubescents are not as advanced as you and have not begun their sexual exploration, so you should not expose them to anything sexual.

Everyone has a right to perfectly normal and safe sexual development that is age appropriate, gender appropriate, and time appropriate. Take your time and be sensitive to others at a different stage than you.

41.   Will I be more creative because I'm gay?

Not necessarily.

Some gay people are very creative and can take part in all forms of the arts, including dancing, acting, directing, choreographing, painting, sculpting, writing, composing music, singing, crafting, and designing.

A lot of gay people hide their sexuality during their teen years, which can help them develop the skill of designing false personas. This experience, which straight people may not have had, may then translate into other creative skills. This could be why gay people are well represented in the art world.

42. Will people be ashamed to associate with me if they know I'm gay?

That depends on their prejudices.

Most people in modern society have accepted that gay people are normal and just want to carry on with their lives like everyone else. Consider racism as an analogy: black people were treated awfully in the past, but now, people of all skin colours are considered equal. That said, some people who perhaps lack education are still racist and bigoted. Those people will pass on their racism to their children, so even now some schoolkids pick on kids who are from ethnic minorities.

While most people treat gay people as equals, unfortunately there is some homophobia (see Q 127) in society. Homophobic people spread false and damaging rumours about the gay community and they try to incite hatred of gay people. They refuse to accept gay people as equals. It is only through the strength and persistence of gay rights campaigns and activism, that these prejudiced people will eventually discover that gay people are equal in every way to everyone else in society.

The gay community will not allow its members to be treated as inferior, and you should remain strong and rely on your supports if anyone harasses you about your sexuality.

Most people will still associate with you in school, college, and at work if they learn that you're gay because most people are educated and smart enough to treat everyone equally. Some people even consider it cool to have gay friends. Not everyone is like this, but do you really want to hang out with people who treat others unequally? Stay strong if people show you bitterness, and rely on your friends that support you.

43.   What if people at school find out that I'm gay?

Your sexuality is your business, and you can choose whom to tell about it. It is useful to talk with the school counsellor or a teacher you trust if you want to offload concerns you have about your peers' thoughts. That adult should keep your confidence.

You have the same rights as everyone else, and you should not have to face any negativity as a result of being gay.

However, some bullying is a part of the culture at any school, and kids who are seen as different whether because of their height, weight, hair colour, skin colour, or sexuality, usually experience some ribbing. You may hear kids using slang names for gay males such as *fag, faggot, bum chum, queer, bender, poofter, gayboy, homo, sausage jockey, pansy, nancy boy, shirtlifter,* and *fairy*. You may also hear derogatory terms for lesbians such as *dyke, butch, lesbo, muff diver, lezzie, leso, todger dodger* and *carpet muncher*. A myriad of other derogatory terms also exist, and more graphic ones are coined every day.

The strange thing is that the people who become the most enraged by gay people are usually uncomfortable with their own sexuality. When they have to face someone who forces them to think about their sexuality, they act out so that others do not pick up on their own issues.

Getting teased in school can be hard, and it's important that you report any bullying to the principal or your year head so it can be dealt with in accordance with the school's anti-bullying policy.

You may find comfort in a group for gay youths where you live. In such a group, you can find out how others deal with homophobic bullying and how you can avoid confrontations with the bullies in your school. *See www. kidpower.org and resources section.*

Your school should have an equality policy that dictates how the principal or year head should deal with students who give others a hard time. You should not have to feel like you're different just because you're gay. You are a good and worthwhile person who happens to be gay. If you feel comfortable doing so, you can educate others that your sexuality is only a part of you and not all of you.

If you decide to come out at school, most people will see this as a positive thing and will probably admire that you're willing to stand up for yourself and that you're proud to be gay.

In general, gay people who are out are less likely to be bullied about their sexuality, as controlling your disclosure and accepting yourself, disarms the bullies. However, such disclosure doesn't suit everyone. Some people prefer to keep the information to their close friends, and others choose not to tell anyone, although keeping the information a secret can make dealing with it a lonely experience.

44.   Will my school cover homosexuality in sex ed?

It depends on your school.

Some religious schools do not acknowledge that a proportion of students may be gay. In such a school, the sex ed curriculum will focus on relationships between men and women and on pro-creation within these heterosexual relationships.

In more liberal and forward-thinking schools, sex ed will discuss gay relationships and the sexual activity between gay people. If your sex ed class does not discuss gay relationships, you might consider talking to the sex ed teacher about this. If enough people advocate for a more inclusive curriculum, homosexuality and gay relationships might be included in these classes in the future.

45.   Why do gay kids get bullied?

Anyone who is part of a minority group can be a victim of bullying. This goes for people who are disabled, who are from an ethnic minority, or who are cross-eyed, big-eared, small, tall, large or skinny.

Kids who are gay are different to most kids. Some gay kids are gentler and more sensitive than other kids, and these other kids may see this as strange and not know how to react. If a kid has been bullied at home or comes from an otherwise violent or unsettled family situation, he or she may seek out targets for their anger and become bullies. Unfortunately, these targets are often gay kids.

You do not have to accept being bullied. Schools in many countries now have anti-bullying policies, and many principals and year heads have had specific training about anti-gay bullying. If you're bullied, be sure to tell a trusted adult or parent about it.

Gay students often find that life is much easier after they've disclosed that they're gay. Kids may fear coming out because they think they'll receive an endless tirade of bullying, but in fact, the opposite seems to happen, as bullies no longer have the power to out these kids and are therefore disarmed. Also, when you're in control of your situation and are proud of being gay, bullies have nothing to taunt you about.

You have rights, and you don't deserve to be bullied. Stand up for yourself. You deserve to be happy.

46.   Do I have to follow a gay lifestyle if I'm gay?

There is no single definition of what a gay lifestyle is, so your lifestyle, whatever that is, will be a gay lifestyle. You have the freedom to live your life as you see fit.

What is traditionally considered a gay lifestyle is changing all the time. When the gay movement was hidden away from mainstream society, gay people tended to be more flamboyant when they came together, as they were often exhausted from keeping up a straight facade in everyday life. So, many people minced around and participated in overt camp activities.

Nowadays, however, gay people do not have to limit being openly gay to particular nights or outings with their gay pals. Gay people now just act, look and participate like everyone else, in all the usual activities that are just part of normal life.

Some people think that the gay lifestyle involves lots of booze, drugs, and sexual activity and that gay people only wear designer clothes and go on expensive holidays. This just isn't the case for the majority of gay people, as they cannot all afford such extravagances and realise that booze and drugs will negatively affect their health.

The media tends to portray the extremes of any minority group as the norm, but most gay people live perfectly normal lives. They live in normal houses, wearing normal clothes, and eat normal food; they have the same amount of sexual encounters as everyone else; and they go on holiday to the same places as everyone else. Gay people are not particularly identifiable on the street or in the workplace, and more often than not, they are in perfectly normal, functional relationships with their partners.

47.   Have I different DNA or a different genetic code if I'm gay?

Many studies have been done on the genetic make-up of gay people, particularly on siblings, to answer this question. No one has yet discovered a gene that absolutely determines whether someone is sexually and romantically attracted to people of the same gender.

Some studies have found that a higher proportion of gay people than their heterosexual counterparts carried the gene code Xq28. Scientists are still debating this matter, however, as not all gay people carry this gene. So, there is no proof that gay people have a particular genetic pattern.

48. If I hide the fact that I'm gay, does that make me dishonest?

No.

Deciding whether to tell someone you're gay or to keep your sexuality to yourself is your choice. If you're not ready to tell others about your orientation, you're entitled to keep a lid on it.

Your circumstances and surroundings are unique to you, and when you disclose your sexuality, most people will understand that this was something you needed time to come to terms with for yourself, first.

49. If I am gay, can I force myself to be sexually attracted to someone of the opposite gender?

No.

There have been many attempts to turn people straight using a variety of therapies and brainwashing programs, but none of them have worked.

50. If I have sex with someone of the opposite gender, will I become straight?

If you're gay, you're gay.

If you are bisexual, you may find that you're more strongly drawn to a particular gender if you happen to fall in love with someone of that gender. This may then change if that relationship ends and you begin another relationship with someone of the other gender.

If you're gay and you have sex with someone of the opposite gender, this will not affect your natural sexuality. You may be the most powerful (or hopeless) lover that person has ever had, but you will find that you're still attracted to people of the same gender as yourself afterwards.

51. Do I need counselling if I'm gay?

Not necessarily.

Some people feel that counselling helps them to deal with a variety of issues in their lives, and until you become comfortable with being gay, it may be an issue you wish to talk about in counselling.

Counselling helps us talk through difficulties and to understand why we do what we do and why we think the way we think. It can help to unknot some of the troubles of the mind and free us up to live authentic lives.

Many teenagers speak with their school counsellor, but you can also speak with your parents or another adult whom you know will hold what you say in confidence.

52. I have so many mixed feelings about being gay. Is this normal?

Absolutely.

Many people who discover that they're gay want to become straight, as they're afraid of their feelings, which may seem at odds with how their friends are feeling. Some people find it hard to accept that they're gay and think, "why me"?

This is perfectly normal and natural. You'll eventually become more comfortable with the idea and realise that it's a part of your nature and something that you cannot change. However, it takes time to come to terms with the enormity of this part of your make-up.

Because of the community and society they live in, some people find it really difficult to accept that they're gay. This can lead to *internalised homophobia (see Question 130).*

They may like everything about themselves except that they're gay. They may feel like their minds are split because they love themselves but hate this part of who they are. Internalised homophobia is destructive, and it can keep people from loving their whole beings. This may also lead them to be intolerant of other homosexuals. They may even be the most outspoken homophobes in their surroundings.

If you feel this way, seeing a counsellor or talking to a trusting adult can help you to deal with every aspect of your life, allow you to see that being gay is okay, and to help you live authentically.

53. Whose business is it if I'm gay?

No one but your own.

You don't have to reveal your sexuality to anyone if you choose not to, just as straight people don't have to come out of the heterosexual closet.

However, if you do wish to be authentic to yourself and others, you may choose to tell one person, everyone you know, or a selection of those around you. It's your decision, and no one has the right to force you to say anything.

In most circumstances, it's best to let some people know that you're gay so that you can be yourself sometimes and not have to be concerned all the time about keeping your secret.

54. I'm gay, but I am not the sporty type. My dad insists on making me train for a sport I hate. What can I do?

Most teenagers feel a tension between their desire to feel protected by their parents and their desire to burst into adulthood and make their own decisions. This can come about in cases when parents have pushed hobbies on teenagers because parents feel that these activities will be good for their children's development.

If a father notices his son exhibiting characteristics that fit gay stereotypes, he may try to push his son to participate in activities that fit masculine stereotypes. The father may do so in a misguided effort to reverse his son's nature and to toughen him up to fit the father's image of masculinity.

When you find yourself in this situation, you might consider being honest with him that you do not want to continue with the activities he has chosen for you, and you may also wish to be honest with him about being gay. He may seem disappointed or even angry at first, but he will probably come around when he understands you better, and he'll stop pushing you to do something that you don't want to do.

If you think he'll be unable to accept that you are gay, you may need to put your foot down and explain firmly that you do not enjoy the sport, that you hate the training, and that you do not wish to continue. This may lead to an argument and even a stand-off, but most dads don't want their kids to be unhappy, so if he's in any way reasonable, he'll let it go.

If your relationship with your dad is close enough, you can be open with him about which activities you prefer and inform him that the activity he's chosen for you isn't for you and that you want to try other things.

With all that said, sports are positive activities for all people to engage in. If you don't like a particular sport, perhaps you should try others to see which ones suit you.

Some gay people have avoided team sports because they feared awkwardness in the dressing rooms. However, this attitude is changing as more and more professional sportspeople come out as being gay, and it is becoming easier to be gay in a team environment as time goes on.

55. If I fantasise about someone of my own gender, am I gay?

Not necessarily.

Boys and girls often go through a period in adolescence when they fixate on someone that they admire. This could be a pop star, movie hero, sporting hero, gaming hero, or popular person in his or her school, family, or community. People who have such an infatuation sometimes copy that person's habits, style, desires, or aspirations. They might confuse their admiration with love and fantasise about being that person or being with that person. Such feelings are normal and do not mean that the person who feels them is gay.

That said, if you are gay, you might fall in love with someone you know or a celebrity who is the same gender as you are. You may have sexual feelings for and fantasies about this person. You might dream about this person.

If you only fantasise about people of your own gender, then it is likely that you are gay. If you fantasise about people of both genders about equally, you may be bisexual.

56. What about my body image?

Some people believe that gay people are more body conscious than other people. This is not necessary so.

Gay men who are "bears" promote a traditionally masculine macho look. They are generally men who are stocky and hairy and they believe in the acceptance of all types of bodies.

Images of homosexuals as slim, feminine-looking men or butch, chubby women are stereotypes that are still promoted in the media. But gay people come in every shape, size, and form. Be comfortable with whatever body nature has provided for you.

57.   Can I be successful as a gay person?

Absolutely.

Gay people are found in every walk of life, from billionaires to beggars, so anything is possible.

If you define success as having a lot of money, then you'll find that gay people generally do well in their jobs. They might be more flexible in their work hours than their straight colleagues because they may not have to rush off to crèches or children's activities. They may also be able to travel more readily than others who have more home commitments.

Gay people often merge their careers with the rest of their lifestyles and spend a lot of their time mixing the social and professional aspects of their careers.

People also define success in other ways that have nothing to do with money, too. Success for others is about personal achievement and is not measured in terms of business turnover, customer numbers, units of sales, or social media followers.

Success is finding a balance in life and feeling fulfilled by your activities, both personal and professional. This fulfilment comes from feeling like you're contributing to society, pushing yourself to achieve what you can, remaining loyal to those who love you, being creative, keeping fit, maintaining financial security, and above all, being true to yourself and enjoying this one shot you have at life.

If you have all this or are on the road to achieving it, then you should consider yourself a success.

58. Can I do any job I like if I'm gay?

Yes.

Our society has stereotyped gay people into certain jobs, but gay people perform every type of job imaginable, in every industry, and at every level. Gay people are not bound by stereotypes anymore, so you should pursue the career that feels right for you, irrespective of your sexuality.

59. Will life be more difficult because I'm gay?

Your life will not necessarily be more difficult than someone else's just because you are gay or straight. Your difficulties or successes in life are a result of your choices for how you live your life.

In adulthood, when you manage to get away from the immature bullies that you find in school, you're free to do as you wish. You're protected by law in most countries from homophobic discrimination, so you can't be denied a job, entry to a bar or club, a service, membership to a group, or participation in other activities just because you're gay. Civil society has come to embrace gay people, and most barriers to living your life to the fullest have been removed.

You might not have biological children as a gay person, and some people see this as having a void in their lives. If you feel this way, you can choose surrogate parenting, fostering, or adoption. That said, some gay people say that they don't wish to be parents, and they're perfectly happy living their lives without children.

Some gay people feel that they would be better off being straight, but this wish does little to ease their paths through life. If you spend your life yearning for an impossible dream, you will eventually realise that you've wasted your life looking for the greener grass, allowing opportunities to pass you by. There's no point in wondering whether life would be better if you were straight. You have to face facts and live the life you have as well as you can. We only have one go at life, so take every opportunity to squeeze in as many positive life experiences that you can, out of your time here on earth.

Life is all about ups and downs – that's true for everyone. When you experience the downs, don't waste your time blaming something or someone else for them. This only labels you as a victim, which can crush your soul. Instead, take responsibility for both the ups and the downs in your life. Recognise the ups as achievements, and view the downs as lessons. Never allow yourself to become a member of the "just-my-luck" brigade. Doing so causes you to form a negative self-image, and you'll find it difficult to succeed.

We all experience successes, mishaps, wins, losses, victories, defeats, good luck, bad luck, fortune, and misfortune. That's life. Define yourself by how you celebrate your wins and are dignified in defeat.

Today, embrace that being gay is part of who you are, go out and make the most of it, and stop wondering if life would be different if you were otherwise. Be proud to be gay!

60. I feel like I'm the only person who is gay. Are there other gay people around?

Yes.

When you're learning to deal with being gay, you might feel like you're the only one going through this experience. Everyone else may seem to know exactly what they're doing, where they're heading, and who they're attracted to.

This couldn't be further from the truth. If you are a teenager, the other teenagers around you may seem to have life sorted, but secretly, they all have questions about who they are, what they should be doing, what others are saying, whether they look sorted on the outside, and so on.

Also, between 5 and 10 per cent of all people are gay, so no matter how few gay people there may seem to be around you, there are around 700 million other gay people throughout the world, going through the same thing as yourself. Remember, too, that gay people don't come with labels, so it's not always possible to tell who else is in your situation.

Bear in mind that more people around you than those your own age may be gay. Gay people will also be among your teachers, employers, religious group, family members, neighbours, friends, politicians, workers, teammates, and classmates.

61.   Okay, I'm gay. When should I start dating?

During puberty, it's natural to be inquisitive about what all this sex stuff is about. People at school might say that they're having sex, and it may suddenly seem that everyone is having sex except you. In truth, most of your schoolmates are in the same boat as you and likely aren't any wiser about romance than you are.

Curious boys and girls will start exploring what's going on in their developing minds and bodies around age fifteen or sixteen (although a few might start a bit sooner). This age may be different for boys and girls, and it can also be different for straight sex or gay sex.

You may also wish to engage in these games. If you do, it's important to observe your country's laws regarding the age of consent, which is the age at which you're legally allowed to have sex. You also need to observe your family's rules about dating. These rules apply equally to gay and straight children.

By the age of seventeen, you're likely to have contemplated dating someone. At first you may be interested in dating because you think it'll make you seem grown-up, but in reality, young teenagers are usually reluctant to give up their freedom and commit to a relationship.

62.   Is there any loss associated with being gay?

It depends on your attitude about your sexuality. If you accept the fact that you're gay and live your life exactly as you wish, then you'll have a fulfilling life.

If you want something in your life, go and get it, but be sure you've carefully considered why you want it. If you wish for something just because you think it might impress your neighbours or friends, you'll never be truly happy. In general, other people don't care about you as much as you might think. Instead, please yourself, and let others engage in frivolous one-upmanship.

If you don't have the drive to have children, then you won't lose out by not having them. Some people may feel that not having children is a loss, but if you don't have a parental drive, then you won't feel such a loss.

You might experience the loss of a friendship if your friend does not accept that you're gay, but perhaps such a person wasn't a suitable friend for other reasons, too, and you'll more than make up for it with new friends in the gay community.

You might feel that you've lost your identity for a period in your teens as you come to terms with being gay. In the five-year gap between when most people realise they're gay (around age twelve) and when they feel comfortable telling others about it (around age seventeen), they may lose out on a lot because they feel confused, lonely, shameful, guilty, frightened, or isolated. If this has been your experience, your family, culture, religion, or community may not be making this time any easier. You may find that you have difficulty concentrating and performing well academically.

You may lose out on some family relationships if your family members don't accept that you're gay. However, you will be able to get past these challenges.

It's important that you seek out support from a youth group for gay teens or from a school counsellor or other trusted adult to help you work through all the emotions and anxieties you feel because of any losses you perceive. *See resource section.*

63.   Will I be lonely?

The gay scene is a great place to make friends and to meet potential partners. Most large towns and cities have youth groups for LGBT teens and young adults, and you can find many online support sites aimed at gay people of every age. *See resource section.*

For adults, there are professional dating agencies, online dating sites, and groups for members of the gay community to engage in any hobby or interest.

That said, you do not have to join activities specifically for gay people to make friends or meet partners. Gay people are everywhere, and the potential to make friends is everywhere. Not all of your friends will be gay, and you may have more straight friends than gay ones.

When you feel you're ready to settle down but have difficulty finding a partner, you may be lonely for periods, but there is someone for everyone, and sometimes you have to kiss a few frogs before you find your Prince or Princess Charming.

Many gay people find it easier to find one-off sexual mates than partners, but if you really want love, make that known (and treat people with respect and dignity) then love will find you.

64.   Is being gay a medical thing?

No.

It is an emotional and physical part of your life. Medically, gay people's bodies operate the very same as everyone else's.

65.   Is being gay a psychological thing?

Being gay isn't a psychological condition, but every aspect of our existence has a psychological dimension. Being gay is a fact of life and at the core of your existence. It is not just something in the mind.

You will find that when you're attracted to someone of the same gender, your genitals, heart, blood, and senses will be as active as your mind is, as you consider what you desire from that person.

66.   Is being gay illegal?

In most developed countries, no.

Sexual activity between consenting adults is legally allowed in most countries, but you must ensure that you are of legal age in order to engage in sexual acts.

In some developing countries, sexual relations with another person of the same gender is still illegal. These tend to be more conservative countries where education is controlled by the dominant religious group and the laws are determined by the dominant religion. Uganda (for example) has particularly tough laws around homosexual activity.

In these countries, people may face court proceedings, prison sentences and even the death penalty for having sex with someone of the same gender. However, if the punishments are severe, it is likely that the leaders of other, more developed countries, will condemn them as discriminatory and threaten legal sanctions such as trade embargoes, if gay people are not given equal rights and protection.

If you are travelling abroad, it is wise to research in advance what the local people consider appropriate behaviour regarding public displays of affection and whether the country has strong views on homosexuality.

67. Is being gay immoral?

No.

However, it is unhealthy to deny your true nature whether you are straight or gay. You need to be true to yourself so you can fully live your life.

Some religions are beginning to claim that they are accepting of gay people in their congregations. They know that there are gay people everywhere, and if they condemn homosexuality, they know that they ostracise gay people and their supporters. Most religious leaders will say that they do not have any problem with gay people, and some may even be gay themselves. They are expected to follow the rules of their faith, and in many cases, one of these rules is that all sex outside of marriage is immoral.

The vast majority of people have learned from the heterosexual community that not allowing people to have sex can be damaging and that it is natural to want to have sex once you reach sexual maturity.

In time, religions who hold views against homosexuality may decide to update these views, as they cause the religions to lose followers. As people become more educated, they realise that such old-fashioned thinking is unfair to the sectors of society that it affects, and religious teachings that are unfair to gay congregants may also change because followers and leaders recognise this.

You'll develop your own moral code over time, and you should live by it. This is likely based on the sense of right and wrong that your family instilled in you, but as you grow, you'll adapt it to your own comfort zone in other areas of life. You'll probably have fine-tuned your moral code by the time you're in your late twenties or early thirties, so there's no need to panic if you're not yet sure what is right for you just yet.

68.   Is being gay a sin?

No.

Most religions say that people are born in the likeness of their creator who controls the whole universe, so this means the creator is responsible for your sexuality along with everything else.

Some religions say that acting on your homosexuality is a sin, but by the same token, they also say that sex before marriage is a sin.

Masturbation is considered a sin in some religions, but science has proved that masturbation is a natural activity that's useful for relieving sexual frustration and expelling unused sexual fluids.

You need to decide this issue for yourself, but in my view, if you're being true to yourself as someone who is gay and if have a natural sexual desire, acting on that desire within appropriate boundaries is not a sin. If you believe in a higher being that created you, then know that this higher being understands and loves all of you!

69.   I'm a Christian. Will I go to hell because I'm gay?

No.

If you can accept the fact that being born gay was not a choice you made or something you set out to do, then this means that you were born gay as a result of something natural. Most religions state that we are born in the likeness of the creator. So, if your creator has created you as a gay person, then your creator must be okay with that.

Somewhere along the line, members or leaders of various religions have tried to make out that being gay is wrong. They simply have not understood that being born gay is a natural phenomenon and not that person's choice.

When people accept this fact, they see that it's ridiculous to discriminate against gay people. They don't understand that doing so is like telling a person he's wrong because he's disabled or telling someone else she's wrong because of the colour of her skin or telling a another person that they're wrong for being small.

In all these situations, it was nature that dictated that these people be born with whatever sexual orientation, disability, skin tone, hair colour, birthmark, height, or other unique quality.

So accept that you're gay as a result of how nature has created you. No creator can turn their own creations away because of something the creator is responsible for.

70.   Do I have to dress a certain way to be a real gay?

No.

Dress the way you feel most at ease dressing.

Some people want to buy into the fashion of the gay scene, and this tends to be at the cutting edge of trends. However, trying to keep up with fashion can be exhausting and expensive, and it's not necessary.

You should wear what feels right for you!

71. How do I tell my grandparents, who are very old-fashioned, that I'm gay?

First, remember that you need to respect your grandparents' beliefs. They may have been brought up in a culture that viewed homosexuality unfavourably and have not changed their minds as society has changed.

You will know if your grandparents will be able to take the news without getting too upset. Sometimes it's better to leave well enough alone. Some people are too entrenched in their beliefs to come around to accepting your sexuality.

Bear in mind, too, that some elderly people are more aware than you might think. Your grandparents might surprise you with their contemporary views. If you tread carefully (maybe gently mention a gay related topic over lunch) you'll learn whether disclosure or nondisclosure is right for you.

It's probably wise to ask your parents about the best approach, as they know their own parents best.

Some gay people have found their grandparents to be their best supporters.

72. Will I be depressed if I'm gay?

Probably not.

As you deal with the realisation that you're gay, you may experience depressive episodes, but these will pass once you learn to accept yourself and accept that being gay is just part of who you are.

Again, talking to your peers or a trusted adult such as a counsellor will help you to negotiate life as a gay person.

73. Is it better to live in the city or the countryside if I'm gay?

Being gay has no bearing on where you live. Where you live depends on what you want to do with your life. A lot of gay people do live in cities, however, as a lot of people like to be connected to a gay scene.

If you feel that being part of a big gay scene is for you, then a city might hold more appeal. However, if you prefer a rural life in the countryside, then country living is for you.

It can be challenging to come out in a rural setting, as people who live in rural areas are traditionally quite conservative. If you do come out in a rural setting and you're the first person in your community to do so, it may take time for the locals to adapt to your status, but if you maintain your dignity, they'll likely come to accept you as you are. You may even become a bit of a celebrity in your town or village for doing so.

You're also likely to be teased by less knowledgeable locals as they struggle to keep up with changing society. This may make you feel unwelcome and may try to challenge you to think about living elsewhere. But if you think about it, these people probably aren't important in your life and do not deserve to affect your thinking about where you should live. The people who are important are the ones that support you. Don't live your life trying to please unimportant people.

74. Will I have a limp wrist?

No.

A limp wrist was a subtle sign that gay people developed decades ago to identify each other when they had to be secretive about being gay. This became a symbol of homosexuality and was used extensively in film and TV for viewers to identify a gay character.

Today, there is no need for this type of overt gesture, but some people still adopt it as a sign to show the world that they are gay.

If this gesture feels natural to you, then go for it. If not, then there's no need to adopt it.

75.   Can I have straight and gay friends?

Yes.

In modern society, it is normal for groups of friends to be made up of gay and straight people. If you are gay, it's healthy to have both gay friends and straight friends so that you gain from all of their life experiences.

76.   My best friend is straight. Will he or she abandon me when I come out?

Probably not.

However, if your bond with your friend is strong, he or she may react negatively to your revelation at first because you hid this secret.

Straight pals may be uncomfortable with the idea because they worry that others will think they, too, are gay. They may need some time to cool off after you come out to get their own heads around the fact they you're gay. They'll probably come around and your friendship may even be better than it was before.

If your friendship does however end just because of your disclosure, you will need to accept that this type of person may not have been healthy for you and that you'll need to make friends with more liberal-minded people.

77. I live in a country where being gay is illegal. Should I move to a more liberal country?

If you're still a minor, your parents are still responsible for you, and it's probably best to live with them until you're old enough to choose where you want to live.

When you reach the legal age of adulthood, your options for where you live are more open. This may mean that you decide that moving away is the best option. Or you may decide to stay because there are many others in your country who are in the same boat as you, and together you can start or join a local group to campaign for change.

As has been mentioned, being gay is not something that you choose, and laws that discriminate against gay people are unfair. Your government needs to change how they treat their gay citizens. Advocating for change can be a slow and tedious process, but change has to start somewhere and with someone!

A group of dedicated gay people and their supporters are necessary to affect change in any country that has had discriminatory laws. You could be part of that change in your country.

If you choose to become an advocate, be careful how you approach the process, and get support from groups in more liberal countries to learn how best to approach the state in order to get a peaceful and amicable outcome for you and your fellow gay citizens. Have a look at *www.frontlinedefenders. org* for support and advice.

78.   I live in a developed and liberal country, but my family are deeply engrained in the religion of our less liberal home country. How do I deal with this?

Some religions view homosexuality as some kind of a curse from the devil. Over centuries, religions have forced negative views about homosexuality on their followers, as they incorrectly deem it to be unnatural.

These religions may have been started by educated people to create fear among the uneducated people in their communities because a lot of people in ancient times followed barbaric practices. They needed something higher than humans to dictate that they act ethically and morally. However, in contemporary society, we are more educated and understand that we cannot all do whatever pops into our minds. We have laws and other codes to keep us in check.

We are all sexual beings driven by our nature to have sex. We've created laws about sex regarding the age of consent and what we consider acceptable and unacceptable behaviour. These laws include punishments for breaching these rules.

According to the law in most Westernised societies, being gay is fully acceptable, as these societies recognise that some people are just born gay. So, as long as gay people's sexual activities happen between consenting adults (those old enough to legally consent) in a private place, then away they may go.

Many religions have not yet adopted such leniency or acceptance, and some still demonise homosexuality. Some religious people don't believe their children when they come out as gay – they simply can't believe that this is possible.

As mentioned earlier, some religions now say that they accept gay people but don't condone the sexual acts between homosexuals. This is both confusing and discriminatory.

Ironically, it is statistically probable that some people in the hierarchy of every religious community are themselves gay. They may have even chosen their vestments to avoid dealing with their sexuality. Therein lies one of the challenges to changing these unaccepting religions.

If your family hold fundamentalist beliefs, they may find it difficult to accept that you're gay. They may need extra support and perhaps counselling to come to a place of acceptance.

With all that being said, you may decide that the fight is not worth it. You may have to leave well enough alone and live your gay life separately from your family life. This is a less than ideal situation, but sometimes you need to choose your battles carefully in order to get the most from your life.

If you know in your heart of hearts that you won't win this fight with your family, it may be too much for you to take on, so not disclosing your sexuality to them may be in the best interest of all concerned. It is a pity, but that may be your reality.

However, even staunchly religious people sometimes come to accept their family members' being gay, and it may be possible for you to break through your family's prejudices with the right amount of persistence, defiance, dialogue, patience, and persuasiveness.

79. I'm straight, but I've just learned that my best friend is gay. Will people think I'm gay as well?

No.

Childhood friends have to deal with changes in each other as they go through puberty. Many of your friends could turn out to be different to you, and these differences only become apparent when you reach sexual maturity.

A friend who tells you that they are gay respects you enough to confide in you. Your friend may have been on tenterhooks for a long time before making the disclosure as they sought the best way to tell you. Your gay friend has been going through a lot to figure it all out, and right now, they need your support.

This is a test of your friendship and is new territory for both of you. It can be a difficult time. It is natural to feel shocked and confused and to have a lot of questions. Ask your friend whatever you feel you need to ask. You may wonder if your friend fancies you, and perhaps he or she does. However, if a gay person fancies you, that doesn't mean that you're gay – it just means that you're attractive. Hey, if a gay person finds you attractive, others will too. Remember that it's rare for people to think that you're gay just because your friend is gay, just as people won't think you're blind if you hang around with a friend who is blind.

You should just carry on doing your own straight thing by dating, flirting and whatever comes naturally to you.

Reassure your best friend that you'll stick by him or her as he or she comes to terms with being gay, and if you need time to deal with the news, be honest with your friend.

When you demonstrate that you stick by your friends no matter what their sexual orientation, you demonstrate your strength and loyalty, and these are attractive features.

80. I heard that someone used to be gay but is now straight. How did this happen?

Sometimes people who are gay act as though they're straight, and sometimes people who are straight act as though they're gay.

For all kinds of reasons, gay people often lead straight lifestyles until they're ready to come out. When they do, those around them usually understand that they have always been gay and just waited for the right time to come out.

However, when people who have said that they're gay come out as being straight, the situation is not always so clear-cut. They may have always been straight and were just experimenting with gay life. If so, this doesn't mean they were gay and then turned straight. Instead, it means that they discovered their true nature in the end.

Sometimes after weighing up their options, gay people decide that they want to live straight lifestyles and have families with members of the opposite gender. This doesn't mean that the gay people have turned straight; it just means that they chose a straight lifestyle. A gay politician may decide that living a straight lifestyle is the best way to get or keep votes. A gay businessperson may feel that a straight lifestyle may help him or her look like a stereotypical citizen to his or her business community.

As society changes, fewer people feel it necessary to engage in this type of deception, but it still happens. A gay person living a straight lifestyle will still have the sexual urges and desires of a gay person, so this choice often leads to unhappy marriages and difficult family situations.

However, heterosexual spouses of gay people who are fully informed of their spouses true sexuality may decide to facilitate their gay spouses' wishes to keep up appearances and live their lives as soul mates rather than bona fide lovers. Heterosexual spouses may also have an understanding if their gay partners stray from time to time to fulfil their natural sexual needs. These relationships can be positive if everyone knows where they stand and no one is deceived.

81. I don't fit the stereotype of gay people that I see on TV. Might I not be gay?

The media have traditionally presented gay men as camp, effeminate, slim, attractive and dramatic and usually try to portray lesbians as stern, masculine and tough.

These stereotypes have caused confusion for people exploring their sexual identities. Gay people can fit these images, but they can also be large, small, pretty, ugly, burly, delicate, deep voiced, timid, tall, short, fat, thin, exciting or boring.

The media are slowly changing this narrow image and showing that gay people, like straight people, come in all shapes and forms, all levels of intelligence, all ethnic backgrounds, all personalities, and all levels of attractiveness.

82.   Are there support groups I can join?

Many support outlets and forums are available to gay people. You can join a youth group or other organisations for teens (and adults) dealing with coming out. Each area is different so I suggest you search online for your nearest ones. You might be surprised how close and available support is to you.

Online groups and forums also exist for users to discuss the queries, concerns, joys, milestones, and accomplishments that they encounter on their journeys of dealing with being gay.

For a list of LGBT Rights organisations who can point you towards the supports close to you, have a look at the resource section at the back of this book.

83.   Where can I get more information about and support for being gay?

Major towns and cities in most Western societies have gay support centres. If you don't feel comfortable going to the one closest to you, get in touch with one in another place.

These centres usually provide details for support groups appropriate for your age, literature about sexual health, and information about activities, events, campaigns, and laws relevant to your situation. *See resource section.*

Questions from the Family of a Gay Person

84.   How do I cope with having a gay child?

Parents often have some indication that their children are gay before they know for sure. These children may act differently to their brothers or sisters and have very different ideas about love and relationships.

Do what you can to ensure that your children know that they can approach you about anything. Don't allow family members or others in your social circle to make homophobic comments, and ensure you drop into conversations, phrases and comments which indicate that you're understanding of gay people. Doing so will let your child know that he or she will be accepted in the family if he or she comes out as gay.

Teenagers will pick up on their parents' views of gay people, and if these are negative, teenagers might move out before they're ready, never disclose their true identities, turn to alcohol or drugs, or even end their life through suicide. Such outcomes are tragic in every way and wholly avoidable.

Let your children know that you would still love them and that they would still be members of the family if one or more of them turned out to be gay.

When you've left the door open for gay children to disclose their sexuality to you, be ready for the moment when they decide to tell you. Don't be upset if you're not the first person they've told. Teenagers often feel most comfortable approaching a teacher, counsellor, friend, or support group first. This is natural, as teenagers and parents often have a disconnected line of communication, leading teenagers to seek help outwards before turning back inwards.

When you hear the news, react as you would to any emotional disclosure, whether that's with a hug, a kiss, a handshake, or another gesture to ensure your child knows that this news is not going to damage your relationship. Respect your child's decision to wait to tell other members of the family, perhaps even the other parent. They need this time, perhaps to cool off after having told you, as all the emotions attached to such disclosures can be exhausting.

Allow your child plenty of opportunities to have private discussions with you about being gay, and be understanding as he or she presents issues or questions or doubts to you. The topic may change weekly as they adjust.

Try not to treat this child any differently, but don't allow the family to use him or her as a scapegoat or siblings make him or her a victim of bullying or rivalry because of their differences.

If other siblings are being difficult, remind them that their gay sibling is as much a part of the family as everyone else and that each of them is loved and cherished no matter what challenges life throws at them.

Your gay child should be required to adhere to all the rules regarding curfews, age-appropriate activities, dating, sleepovers, and so on that you set for all your children. House rules apply to all children equally.

You may find the adjustment period a lonely time, so get as much support as you can from your family and friends or from a local support group for parents going through a similar situation. *See www.pflag.org and the resource section.*

85. Has something wrong about our parenting style made our child gay?

No.

It is a common misconception that parenting styles can influence a child's sexual orientation. In truth, parents can do nothing to affect whether a child is gay or straight. You can force kids to take part in the most stereotypical activities for their gender, but these won't affect their true sexual identity. The opposite is also true – allowing boys to do ballet and girls to play soccer won't make them gay. People are born gay, straight, asexual, or bisexual (as well as a few variations of these main four).

Children should be encouraged to be true to themselves and should be allowed to follow whatever pursuits best suit their personalities.

Study after study has shown that gay people exist in every facet of society, and the parenting style and presence or absence of one or both parents does not determine the sexuality of their children.

Creative hobbies and interests are healthy for all children, and if they want to do hobbies that are not typical for their gender, these activities will not turn them into tomboys or sissies.

A mother might feel that she has been too protective or overbearing, and a father may feel that he was not a good role model or didn't encourage more gender-appropriate activities. Regardless of parenting styles and activities, people are either gay or they're not.

86. Is having a gay child in the family a problem to be solved?

No.

Some families find it difficult to deal with the idea that one of their family members is gay because it is a relatively new phenomenon for a parent to have to deal with, and the family likely does not have much experience with such a disclosure. People being gay is not the new phenomenon, just coming out about it is.

Some parents do view it as a problem. As a parent, you need to look beyond the fact that your child is gay and see that he or she is still your son or daughter. Acknowledge to yourself, your spouse, and the child that you still love them and care for them.

There are many types of families, and each one has a unique set of characteristics and circumstances. Some families will accept a gay person with open arms, some will do so reservedly, some will need time to adjust before embracing their gay family member, some will remain cautious, and others will reject their family member entirely.

As a parent who hears that your child is gay, you must acknowledge that this is not something your child has chosen and that your child may have been carrying this information around as a secret for some time and felt distress because of it. To hear this news means that your child trusts that you as a parent will support him or her through life and needs your love, support, acceptance, and protection, just as he or she did prior to this disclosure.

87.   As a parent, how can I accept that I have produced a gay child?

This is a big issue for many parents. Traditionally, parents of gay sons or daughters have been led to feel that they are inferior to their peers. Less liberal societies might even expect parents to disown their gay kids in order to save face in the community.

Parents may falsely believe that they have passed down a gene that has produced a homosexual kid. However, your family situation is not unique – gay children exist in a large proportion of families in every corner of the globe. A gay child is not so because of a genetic flaw. Nature has merely created your child with different characteristics to most other children.

Parents of gay children sometimes refuse to accept their child as being gay and may force them to deny their sexuality. This equates to being a form of conditional love, and such a child can never feel fully connected to his or her parents. This can also lead children to follow pursuits that they detest or to form heterosexual relationships that will most likely be dysfunctional. Such children are forced to live a lie and ultimately create an unhappy existence for them, their spouses, and any children they may have. They will likely grow to resent their parents for forcing them into this unhappy situation.

If you fear ridicule from your community for having a gay child and because of this, raise your child according to dogma from your society, you rank your neighbours' approval over your child's happiness. If you think about it, you'd be driving your family apart to please a society of ill-informed, loosely connected people that will not be there for you when you need support the most. If you really value your family, you'll see that you have to accept all your children equally and that you need to prioritise your family over your friends and other community members. You may wish to work to change the culture you live in to accept gay people as equally as they do other community members.

Stand up and be loyal to your family, and demonstrate the same pride and love for your gay son or daughter as you do for your other kids. By doing so, you'll gain the respect of those in the community that believe in doing the right thing.

Some members of every community are prejudiced, and this can lead family members to keep secrets about themselves, contributing to a culture of unhappiness. Ask yourself whether this is what you want for your family. Is it more important to you to try and portray a perfect image to the community at the risk of driving your family apart? Where do your priorities lie – with your family as a solid unit, or with a prejudiced community?

Who is more important to you – your child or your peers?

88. As a parent, do I have to accept that my child is gay?

You need to accept the fact that your child is gay, or you risk driving him or her away.

Your child is still the person that you brought into this world. Your gay child has not chosen to be so, and you owe it to yourself and to him or her to accept that fact. Read up on the matter, perhaps attend a support group (*see resource section*), ask lots of questions, talk to lots of people, and reconcile the idea within yourself.

You may feel guilty for not picking up on signs that your child was struggling, unhappy, or going through a difficult time. You may also feel guilty if your child didn't feel he or she could talk to you sooner, when first noticing that he or she was gay. You may feel sad that you didn't pick up on clues that this child required some additional support or that he or she was lonely in the struggle. This is natural, as you care deeply for this person.

Your child still adores you, respects you, loves you, and copies your example. He or she also still needs your love, security, comfort, protection, scolding, praise, understanding, and, most of all, your support as he or she learns to cope with being gay.

You cannot lay blame for this anywhere. It is a naturally occurring phenomenon in hundreds of mammal species, including humans. There are myriad theories about why it happens, but in the end, it happens.

If you are religious, your religion may have strong views on the issue of homosexuality, and you may find it difficult to reconcile the idea of a gay child with your faith. It's likely that your faith dictates that your creator loves everyone equally, so who are you to condemn one of your own for something he or she did not choose? Some religious teachings are outdated and based on ignorance and fear. Times change, and you have to change with them.

If you have courage and conviction, you may need to lobby the leaders of your faith, so that they may also see that they must adapt to modern, educated thinking and change their organisation to be more inclusive.

89.   As a parent, teacher, or supporter of a family, how do I respond to someone who comes out as being gay?

First, you should feel honoured that this person has chosen you to make such a declaration to, as it means you're someone he or she can trust with something very personal and intimate. This person will have weighed the chances of your rejecting him or her and decided that you are not likely to turn your back on them.

When someone comes out for the first time, they are likely to have reflected on this issue for a long time and have maybe felt pain, anguish, and anxiety before deciding to tell you.

If you suspect someone might make such a disclosure, try not to force the situation, as this person may need some time before he or she actually tells you and will perhaps say he or she has something to say but doesn't know how to say it.

Don't make guesses during the discussion, as this could distract from the real issue, and the person coming out may be offended if you make wrong guesses about possibilities that he or she hasn't even considered. Be patient and wait for them to disclose the information.

Until they are ready, be reassuring and say that you'll support and accept them, whatever they have to say. Then sit back and listen.

Then, when you hear that this person is gay, offer reassurance that they are very brave for facing up to this fact, and remind them that this is normal and natural and that they are just like hundreds of millions of others around the world.

If the person coming out to you is a relative, say that you still love them and will ensure your family will continue to protect them. Also reassure this person that the information will not affect your relationship.

At the end of the conversation, check to be sure that they are safe and well before you leave them, and arrange to have another chat within a day or so. Offer to be with them as they begin to tell others.

90.   Do more gay people than others die by suicide?

This is difficult to determine precisely, as many people who kill themselves do not leave a note or other clues that specify the reasons for their choice. However, sadly, gay people do attempt suicide and harm themselves in other ways more often than their straight peers.

As mentioned in other sections, gay people tend to discover this fact around age twelve and disclose it around age 17. That means that most gay people go through five years of difficulty as they keep their sexuality a secret, and this period coincides with the pressures of puberty, a transition to senior school, and academics. These pressures can lead to feelings of despair and hopelessness and can drive some people over the edge.

Parents need to be keenly aware that this life stage is a very difficult time for all teenagers, but particularly for gay teenagers. The sooner gay teenagers can feel comfortable to tell their secret, the sooner you and others can support them to ensure they stay safe.

Many gay teens are bullied during these years, too, which only adds to the despair. Constantly being ribbed for being gay – before they even have time to accept it for themselves – is exhausting and demoralising. They feel victimised, and may also feel ashamed of themselves for having sexual thoughts about their own gender, for being different to their siblings and friends, and even for disappointing their parents because they are gay.

Teenagers don't have the same concept of time as adults do. They find it more difficult to defer gratification and wish to be happy in the present. When they're going through difficult times, they seek instant solutions.

Teenagers must all be taught that they can get through these tough times, and when they do, they'll have more control and can make decisions that will reward them with happy and contented lives. Things may seem tough during the teenage years, but they get better in adult life.

When people kill themselves, they usually just want to kill one piece of them – such as being gay – but they end up killing everything. This is the real pity. Gay people have so much more to offer than just their sexuality, but everything about them is destroyed by suicide.

The saying "The strongest trees have had to bear the strongest winds" applies in this case. When people have a tough time growing up, they tend to be stronger adults than those who had it easy. So if they can get through the tough teenage years, they'll likely have an advantage in adult life.

It is important that anyone who thinks about suicide confide in an adult or call a helpline. *Go to www.samaritans.org or see Resource Section.*

Problems are temporary – suicide is permanent.

There is a positive solution to any problem, it just takes some patience and perseverance to find it.

91. My child is gay. Has someone interfered with him or her?

Probably not.

Every child is a potential target for paedophiles, but being abused in childhood does not determine someone's sexuality.

News reports have a tendency to highlight the instances of sexual abuse that are homosexual above those that are heterosexual. Some people incorrectly believe that gay people have a disproportionately high number of paedophiles among their numbers, but actually paedophiles have about the same proportion among heterosexuals as homosexuals.

Exposure to sexual behaviour before a person is at the stage of sexual development can be harmful to that person's view of sex and thus affect how he or she participates in sexual relationships later on in life. A good therapist can help a victim of abuse work through the trauma to arrive at a more healthy view of sex.

92. Can sexual abuse make someone gay?

No.

Sexual abuse can however distort a child's thinking. A child who is sexually abused may develop a skewed or altered view of sex in later life. This can affect his or her sexual development and can have a detrimental effect on future relationships.

Children exposed to sexual activity prior to sexual maturity may not understand why adults would perform such acts, and they may lack trust in future sexual partners and be more confused about sex as they mature.

Victims of sexual abuse who become confused about their sexual orientation should seek out therapists either in their schools or in their communities to recover from their abuse and to clarify their true sexual orientation. They may have been gay already and the abuse just happened to be carried out by someone of the same gender.

Every human passes through natural stages of emotional, anatomical, sexual, hormonal, and psychological development as they age. If any of these stages is interrupted by abuse, the abused should get help to attend to that stage, in order to live a balanced life. This is done through counselling or psychotherapy.

Some people who are abused are naturally gay but grow to question whether they're gay as a result of the abuse or whether they would be gay anyhow. Therapy can help these people work through such questions in a structured way within a safe environment.

Whatever the case, all victims deserve the opportunity to heal the wounds they've suffered as a result of the trauma and to carry on into adulthood being true to who they are, whether they're gay or straight.

93.   My son acts like a sissy. Is he gay?

Not necessarily.

On the spectrum of life, everyone has a different set of cells, hormones, chromosomes, DNA and personality traits. No two people are the same and everyone fits somewhere on the continuum from Alfa-male to Alfa-female.

A boy who engages in activities typically assigned to girls may do so simply because his parents have allowed him the freedom to be himself without being constrained by rules of what has been deemed appropriate for males and females.

For too long, males in our society have had to act strong, be emotionless, avoid displays of affection, and keep from crying. These old-fashioned concepts of masculinity have created a difficult situation for men, who need to demonstrate emotions, be romantic, and cry when situations prompt them to.

If your boy is displaying characteristics or preferences that are stereotypically feminine, he may be gay, or he may be straight. He might just be demonstrating that he is comfortable with his emotions and is not afraid to display them or that his skills lie in activities more commonly associated with women than men.

Or, he may act straight and be strong at sports but also be gay. As more and more gay sportsmen and women come out, the world can see that gay people come from all walks of life, are at all levels of ability, and engage in every group, activity, and profession. No particular trait or characteristic defines someone's sexuality or gender.

94.   My 4 year old son likes to dress up in his mother's clothes and plays with girls toys. Will he be gay?

Not necessarily.

Every parent wishes for their children to be happy and healthy. Sometimes, parents require their children to follow traditional gender roles, giving boys blue blankets, football-themed birthday cards and toy cars, and giving girls pink blankets, dolls, and prams.

In truth, toddlers and young children aren't yet consciously aware of their gender identities, and they will naturally be inquisitive about whatever items are lying around the house. Boys may play with their sister's dolls, dress up in either parent's cloths, and display traits that might not be typically associated with their gender. They have yet to be conditioned into thinking about culturally appropriate activities and interest for their gender.

With all that said, some boys who play with dolls will grow up to be gay. That's life!

95.   My daughter is a tomboy. Is she a lesbian?

Not necessarily.

All children go through phases of experimentation, and children of each gender are expected to exhibit certain characteristics determined by their communities.

As people become more educated, their communities are shedding the long-held stereotypes for males and females and accepting more and more diversity.

Your child may be exercising her freedom and individuality by trying out some pursuits and activities that your community has deemed to be more suitable for boys. If your daughter is gay, then so be it. If she's straight, then she'll be straight. Climbing a few trees will not make her a lesbian. If she has been afforded the freedom to experiment with pursuits outside of stereotypical roles for her gender and does turn out to be a lesbian, she will likely be a happy one.

96.   What will I tell the rest of the family?

Gay people sometimes find a protective brother or sister to be the easiest to break the news about their feelings about their sexuality to first. In other cases, the parents are the first port of call. Either way, the gay person should discuss the coming-out process with this trusted family member to decide the best way forward.

Gay people who come out may be surprised by their family's reactions – the ones they thought would be okay with the news may not be, and those they thought would revolt might be their best supporters.

Whatever your reaction, you have to have some time to digest the news. You need to realise the difficulties the gay person went through between their personal discovery and their choice of timing around the disclosure.

A boy who shares a room with his gay brother may feel uneasy once he knows his brother is gay. However, he'll soon realise that his gay brother is still his brother, and they will likely revert to their usual bickering and bonding eventually.

All siblings will need time to adjust, and younger siblings or cousins may be too young to understand now, so a certain level of discretion may be required when discussing the disclosure in their presence.

Elderly relatives may hold strong views about homosexuality, and you may determine that it's not fair to challenge those beliefs if doing so would upset your relative. That said, a lot of older people are more attuned to modern ways than society would have you believe, and grandparents or other elderly relatives could be the greatest allies a gay person in the family could have.

Other extended family members will have many and varied views about someone's disclosing that they're gay. Most will be fine with it, as, like many people, they have gay friends or colleagues. Uncles might tease their brothers about having a gay son or daughter, but most people acknowledge that anyone's kids might turn out to be gay and will be cautious about teasing.

If someone in your family is gay, you need to show them that you support them, no matter what the rest of the family says. As parents, you need to recognise that all your family members are important to you.

97. What'll I say to the neighbours about having a gay child in the family?

This is a private and personal matter, so you're not obliged to say anything about it to the neighbours. You probably don't go into any detail about your own sex life with the neighbours, so why do so with your child's?

People in your neighbourhood may have a particularly conservative view of gay people. For too long, such a view has driven productive gay members out of the community to live elsewhere or caused them to turn to drugs, alcohol, or even suicide. It is time that some people in these conservative communities stand up, cast off these antiquated beliefs, and declare that they are as proud of their gay children as they are of all their children.

Don't allow your neighbours to treat your child any differently to other children, and where appropriate, welcome other gay children in the neighbourhood to your house.

If you really believe that the neighbours will shun your family because one of you is gay, you may need to evaluate whether you really care about what these prejudiced, ignorant people think and whether they're important in your life.

You could keep the information a secret from the neighbours, but if you do so, you may only succeed in driving your child away and shaming him or her, even though he or she had did not choose to have a different sexuality to their peers. You may be left with a rift in the family, an absent (or even dead) child – all to maintain your standing in a prejudiced community.

Who is more important to you, your child or your neighbour?

98. Is there a support group for parents of gay people?

Yes. Parents who live in most Western societies have the option to meet up with other parents to discuss the issues they face as parents of gay children. This often helps parents to come to terms with the idea that one of their children is gay.

A gay child may not have children of his or her own, so parents must deal with the potential loss of the grandchildren that they have hoped for. They may feel guilty if they perceive that they are somehow responsible for their child being gay or simply don't understand how someone could be gay.

When children first tell their parents that they are gay, this brings up many emotions. Parents are often shocked by the revelation and confused about how to handle it.

They need support as they come to terms with the notion that their child is gay, to reconcile any issues this creates with their beliefs, to overcome the myths and stigmas they may have associated with or assigned to gay people, and to deal with their own prejudices about gay people.

Parents also need time to get to know what being gay is all about, time to deal with differences of opinion about the matter between them and their spouses, and time to adjust to the revelation.

With the support of a gay resource centre, parents usually discover that they're not the only ones who have these concerns and that they can support other parents in their journey towards acceptance.

A popular website for Parents and Family/Friends of gay people is *www.pflag.org* and there are other resources at the back of the book.

Questions about the Gay Community and Some Common Terms

99.　What is the gay community?

This is the general term used to describe the gay population within any society. The population is called a *community* because in the past, gay people were not accepted within mainstream life and so created their own community to support each other and validate their sexual identity. For a long time, this was an underground network, and social events would have been held in secret.

Today, the gay community is much more visible in the media and is active in society through entertainment, support groups, education, gay pride/theatre/film festivals, sporting events, political groups, businesses, health clinics, clubs, bars, theatres, resorts, clothing stores, restaurants, LGBT community centers and lots of other services and organizations.

100.　What is the gay scene?

The *gay scene* is all the physical and virtual places where members of the gay community gather to participate in the activities listed in the previous question.

101. What is the gay rights movement?

Gay activities have been recorded in ancient civilisations, indicating that humans have always had homosexual members. When organised religions gained power, society began demonising homosexuals.

Beginning in the 1960s, gay activists resisted the prejudice meted out against members of the gay community. Gay people were constantly harassed by police, and they could take it no more, and in 1969, the Stonewall Riots took place in New York. This turned out to be a most significant uprising and provoked a movement of gay activism.

Gay people realised that nothing was going to change unless they stood up for themselves and showed the world that they are perfectly normal human beings who just happen to be attracted to members of their own gender. They did not have a choice in their sexual orientation, so social attitudes and laws needed to adjust to recognise this fact.

The first gay pride marches took place in 1970, and pride marches and festivals have happened every year since in almost every Western city. Then, in the 1980s, the movement gained mainstream support.

The movement has had many leaders over the years (Harvey Milk being the first to get world recognition) who have inspired millions of dedicated people (of every sexual orientation) to advocate to change legislation to eradicate legal discrimination against gay people.

The gay movement will exist until every gay person in the world is seen as equal. This will take some time!

102. What is a gay rights campaign?

When gay people identify an area where they have been discriminated against or have been treated unequally, they may begin a campaign to change people's views and obtain justice.

These injustices may be cultural, legal, or religious. The campaigns to fight them take many forms, including writing letters to politicians or religious leaders, marches, ad campaigns, publicity stunts or events, demonstrations, political lobbying, and court challenges. Members of the gay community are creative, so there is no end to what approaches they can use.

Some campaigns achieve their goals quickly whereas others require generations to achieve what they set out to do.

103.   What is a gay pride festival?

A gay pride festival is an event held annually in many cities and towns throughout the world. These events began prior to the decriminalisation of homosexuality when a few dedicated gay people paraded through the streets to demonstrate that they were gay, were proud of that fact and that society had better hurry up and accept them. They could not change who they are attracted to, and were fed up with being treated as criminals just for being themselves.

Unease among mainstream society at the sight of these parades led to unrest and violence (as is still the case in some parts of the world), because some people did not like that gay people were advocating for acceptance. However, in western cultures, that acceptance did come about, albeit slowly, as mainstream society saw beyond the sexual act to the people that all the prejudice had been directed towards. As more and more people made their sexuality public, their loved ones were forced to acknowledge that someone close to them had been suffering in silence and that they had participated in the cover-up by not showing their acceptance of gay people.

Gay pride parades grew bigger and bolder each year and eventually included festival floats and a festival atmosphere, which was a departure from earlier activist demonstrations. Current pride events include music, costumes, drag acts, corporate sponsorship, concerts, carnivals, solidarity events, information distribution, discussion, and media coverage. Most of all, they're a celebration of all things gay and a yearly reminder of the journey that gay people have been on to reach the acceptance in mainstream society that they enjoy today.

Everyone is encouraged to take part in the festivals, and while many who attend are themselves members of the gay, lesbian, transgender, and bisexual community, many others are their friends, families, supporters or just partygoers.

104. Are all people who act gay actually gay?

No.

Everyone has unique characteristics and abilities. Some men who are absolutely heterosexual have high-pitched voices or display other qualities typically associated with camp men, and some heterosexual women wear short haircuts and gender-neutral clothing. These outward signs may confuse others and lead them to think that these people are gay when they're not.

By the same token, some gay people sound, look, and behave like the stereotype of a straight person, but they're still absolutely gay.

In truth, there is no way to act gay or straight – the world is moving out of stereotyping and towards an acceptance of androgyny and mixing styles and clothing from all genders.

105. Can gay people be found only in certain parts of society?

Gay people are in every profession, socioeconomic group, club, society, political party, religion, and sport. They are in every culture and are of every colour and nationality. Nature can choose anybody to be gay.

106. Are gay people more sexually active than straight people?

Gay people have about the same levels of sexual urges as straight people, so some have a high sex drive and others have a low sex drive. Men (generally) desire sex more frequently than women so when there are two men in a sexual relationship there is statistically more sexual activity than in a straight relationship.

Lesbian relationships will have slightly less frequency than gay men for sexual activity, but lesbians are generally much more creative, romantic and experimental than gay men.

Because gay people are not universally accepted, they often feel the need to be secretive about their search for a mate so that their families, work colleagues, or community leaders don't find out their true sexuality. This has driven people (generally gay men) to cruise areas where other secretive gay people are known to hang out, and this behaviour may come across as seedy or promiscuous. (See also Q 191 which deals with promiscuity).

107. Is being gay a mental disorder?

No.

Before psychologists discovered that being gay was natural, homosexuality was listed in the *Diagnostic and Statistical Manual of Mental Disorders* (DSM), the standard handbook of psychological disorders. In the 1970s, psychologists finally agreed that homosexuality was not a mental disorder and has no place in this book, so it was removed soon after.

108. What does the word *gender* mean?

Gender describes the characteristics not determined by biology that are considered male and female and assigned to people and things.

Some people who are biologically female may identify their gender as male, and vice versa, and some people do not identify with either gender (See question 113 on *Intersex*).

109.   What is bisexuality?

Someone who is bisexual is physically and romantically attracted to both males and females. This does not mean that they are equally attracted to both sexes, as the attraction to one gender may be dominant over an attraction to the other. Bisexuality has been observed in hundreds of animal species.

110.   What is a transvestite?

A *transvestite* is someone who cross-dresses, or wears the clothes of the opposite gender. This question may perhaps be misplaced in this book, as straight (heterosexual) men are more likely than others to be transvestites.

Many cross-dressing men feel that to dress up in female attire gives them pleasure, as it affords them a psychological break from the endless task of conforming to the stereotype of the rugged male provider. When they are in female clothes, they may feel that they can be more gentle, soft, and nurturing than they can in everyday life. They may feel close to their mothers or other female caregivers when they are in female clothes. Some people cross-dress for fun, and some do so for sexual arousal, particularly when they wear sexy underwear. Even the most macho men might engage in cross-dressing.

111.   What is transgender?

A transgender person is someone who is born with the anatomy associated with one gender but who feels, thinks, acts, and identifies themselves in accordance with another gender.

This is not a new phenomenon, although it is only recently that the world has begun to accept that this is a very real part of some people's identities. The ultimate resolution may be to have sex reassignment surgery (see *transsexual*).

While things are getting easier for transgender people, they are still greatly misunderstood. There is still a social stigma attached to this concept, and parents and friends do not always offer the support that transgender people deserve.

Thankfully, acceptance of the difficulties in the lives of transgender people is growing, and support groups, therapists, surgeons, and services now exist to help them as they consider their options.

If you think that you may be in the wrong body, then you owe it to yourself to look at your options. Seek out the nearest support group and meet others who may be able to help you in your journey.

112.   What is a transsexual?

When a transgender person chooses to reassign their sex – that is, to change their anatomy to match their gender – they are referred to as being *transsexual*.

113.   What does *intersex* mean?

Some people are born with blue eyes, some people are born with black hair, and some people are born with both male and female genitals. Nature has as many ways of creating humans as there are humans. Most people are either male or female, but intersex people are born somewhere in between. It's just nature.

When a child is born intersex, doctors run a series of tests which examine the genitals and reproductive organs, hormones, chromosomes, and blood composition to determine which sex is dominant. Doctors and parents often assign a gender to the child and perform surgery so the child's genitals match that gender. The challenge is that the gender that is assigned may not be the gender that the person will identify with later in life.

If the gender feels natural as the child grows into an adult, there are fewer complications. However, this person may feel that their gender is opposite the gender that they have been assigned – they are transgender. If you have a male body and male genitals and male hormones, everyone assumes you are male. However, if you feel female and think of yourself as a female, then you likely will not feel comfortable living in a male body.

Adults who wish to have bodies that match their minds might choose to have sex-reassignment surgery (see *transsexual*). This can be a difficult, emotional, painful, and prolonged process, but those who complete the process successfully often feel whole and fulfilled and comfortable in their own skin at last.

Some parents of intersex babies choose not to surgically alter their children's genitals so long as they can function normally. So, these children can determine their gender on their own. However, because they might identify as both male and female, and their bodies reflect this, society may need to consider adopting a third gender. *Intersex*, *Genderqueer* and *Non-Binary* are common terms used to describe the third gender identity.

A third gender term would allow people to choose male, female, or a third gender on legal forms, and perhaps in time, we may see three choices for public bathrooms.

114. What is gender expression?

This is dressing or acting like a particular gender. This does not necessarily match a person's biological sex. For example, a boy may choose to express the female gender by wearing make-up and female clothing, and a girl may want to express the male gender by wearing male clothes such as ties and cufflinks. In both situations, this is separate from the person's sexual identity.

115. What is a drag queen or drag king?

Drag queens are men – usually gay men – who dress up as women and provide entertainment. They may perform comedy sketches and mime or sing songs, with a strong preference for big diva numbers. Drag kings are women – usually lesbians – who dress as men and also provide entertainment.

Drag artists can be risqué in their tone in adult bars and clubs, or they can perform family-friendly acts that push the boundaries of gender identity for people of all ages.

116. When two people of the same gender are in a relationship, does one person adopt the role of the opposite gender?

No.

Some people have adopted this misguided concept in an attempt to understand homosexuality. In a gay relationship, each member of the couple will naturally have unique characteristics. Some men are more feminine than others and some women more masculine than others.

Gay couples have to divide up roles and responsibilities in life in order to keep the home and relationship going. Some roles in a household and in life have traditionally been associated with women and some with men. Each gay couple has to decide who does what and sometimes that involves performing tasks not generally associated with their gender.

117. What is asexual?

Someone who is asexual is not sexually attracted to either sex or does not see sex as an important part of life. They usually have a low sex drive and see sex as an option as opposed to a necessary activity.

118. What is the gay or pink press?

This is the name given to publications that deal with issues of interest to the gay community. They can be promotional, commercial, informative, persuasive, advisory, fictional, pornographic, political, gossipy, or antagonistic. Typically, these publications spread information on new findings, research, events, activities, issues, injustices, developments, advertisements, and campaigns happening in the gay community locally and globally.

The Western world has come a long way towards acceptance of homosexuality, and it is important that we support the advance of such acceptance in developing countries as well.

It is important to allow the pink press to report on global developments in order to garner and continue support for people who are still persecuted because of their sexual orientation.

119. What is pink money?

Pink money refers to the spending power of gay people. Because gay people typically do not have to bear the cost of childrearing, they tend to have more disposable income than heterosexuals.

The marketing of goods and services to the gay community has ballooned in recent years as more and more companies try to capitalise on gay people's spending power.

This is also referred to as *The Pink Pound* in the UK or *The Dorothy Dollar* in the US

120. Why do many famous people hide the fact that they are gay?

In the past, most famous gay people hid their homosexuality, but more recently, many have felt able to come out, as being gay is now acceptable to most members of society.

Contrary to what many people would expect, Hollywood has not always been kind to gay actors, and American media in general have been slow to accept homosexuality as a part of life. Gay actors fear that they might be pigeonholed into gay roles only if they come out, as producers may feel that they would not be believable in straight roles.

Many famous people from around the world who wanted to break into the U.S. market have held back on "coming out" just so that they could appeal to Americans. However, this is changing as Americans are now accepting of gay people across the board.

More and more mainstream movies, soap operas, dramas, documentaries, and reality TV shows address the issue of gay people in mainstream life and deal with the old myths and misconceptions about them.

It is no longer a shock or a surprise when famous people come out, and the media are giving less coverage to such stories, so it is likely that more celebrities will be up front about their homosexuality from the beginning of their careers as time goes on.

121. What is a gay scandal?

This is when a tabloid newspaper or trashy magazine "outs" a famous gay person who was pretending to be straight.

When a reporter discovers the celebrity's true sexual orientation (usually because someone has sold the story to the press) they make it out as to be a scandal.

This scandalising does not help the gay movement, as it highlights the fact that some famous gay people think it's better (or better business) to act straight than to come out as being gay.

More and more gay personalities are open from the start of their careers, as doing so saves them the energy of keeping a secret, and they don't have to live in fear of being exposed.

122. Are gay people any good at sports?

They are as good as anyone else.

Many gay people felt isolated in their youth because they feared being outed, and this often led them to avoid taking part in group activities such as team sports and so prevented them from developing their sporting skills.

However, more and more sporting personalities are declaring that they are gay and are met with a very favourable response from the press, their teammates, the gay community, and the public in general.

Some die-hard fans (particularly of football) still find it difficult to accept gay players on their favourite teams, and some of them shout homophobic taunts during matches. This ignorance and bigotry is dying out, but it will take some time for it to disappear. As the saying goes, "Being gay is not a choice, but being a bigot is."

Many sports groups exist specifically for gay people, and they usually compete in mainstream leagues, and are every bit as good.

Gay people also participate in local, national, and international specific gay sporting events, such as the Gay Games and the Out Games.

I encourage everyone to take part in sports, as it's just as important for gay people to stay fit and healthy as it is for everyone else.

123. Why are gay people called *queens*?

The term *queen* is short for *drag queen*, a performance artist – usually a gay man – who masquerades as a woman. *Queen* can also refer more generally to someone who is very feminine and camp. It is mostly used in an affectionate manner now and is no longer seen as derogatory.

124. What does *coming out* or *coming out of the closet* mean?

This is the term used to refer to gay people when they begin telling others that they are gay.

Being in the closet is a metaphorical term for hiding one's sexuality.

When you come out of the closet, you are declaring to others that you are gay. Most people who do so usually feel tremendous relief, for being in the closet can be very lonely, as it leaves you to deal with your sexuality alone.

125. What is a dyke?

This is a pejorative word used to describe a lesbian, particularly one who is masculine or butch in appearance.

126. Why are gay people called "friends of Dorothy"?

Sections of the gay community enjoy musicals, and the movie *The Wizard of Oz* is a particular favourite. Judy Garland had the lead role as Dorothy, and she particularly appealed to members of the gay community.

This descriptor was not widely known among the heterosexual community, so gay people used it as code, asking "Are you a friend of Dorothy's?" to confirm in mixed company whether someone might be gay.

127. What is homophobia?

Homophobia is a prejudice against gay people. This can come from religious or cultural beliefs and is always the result of a lack of understanding. People who are homophobic do not accept that homosexuality is part of normal life and usually think that being gay is somehow wrong.

They tend to discriminate against gay people by spreading rumours and falsehoods about gay people and their activities and blocking changes to laws that recognise gay people as equal. These people usually do not know or accept family, friends, or colleagues who are gay, and they have a narrow view of life. If they could grasp the concept that gay people are just born this way, they would realise that their opposition to gayness is fruitless and their reasoning for it invalid. They would realise that their prejudice is similar to a prejudice against disabled people or Black people. In fact, many homophobic people are also racist.

Ironically, a lot of homophobic people might be battling with their own sexuality. They may think that by proclaiming that they are against homosexuals, others will not suspect that they are gay.

There have been huge swings in positive support for gay people, but perhaps a portion of society will always be homophobic.

128. What is internalised homophobia?

As a result of negative messages or a persistent lack of acceptance of homosexuality from their families, cultures or religions, gay people often internalise a hatred of themselves for being gay. This is a really difficult situation for anyone to find themselves in, as they did not choose to be gay and cannot escape the fact that they are gay.

In order to live a fulfilled life, gay people need to accept they're gay and aim to lead a life that is true to who they are. This may mean that they need to compartmentalise their lives in order to stay connected to a group such as family, work colleagues, or a religious congregation until these groups catch up with the rest of the developed world.

Gay people are often pleasantly surprised by their peers' acceptance when they come out as being gay, and the fear that they will be ostracised by society does not always come true.

129.   Why do some religions not accept gay people?

Religious fundamentalists often believe that their creator dislikes homosexuals.

As mentioned elsewhere in this book, some Christian denominations now say that they accept that some of their members might be homosexuals, but their messages regarding acceptance are confusing and inconsistent.

Some more extreme religions condemn homosexuality, and they will take much more time to reach acceptance. Such an extreme view is often held in theocratic (religious laws and state laws are the same) countries where these flawed beliefs are engrained in people's psyches.

As more and more people become educated, the injustice of discrimination against gay people will change, even among fundamentalists. That may yet be a few generations away in some countries, but it will happen.

130.   What are bears, cubs, otters and wolves?

Bears are gay men who portray a masculine image. Traditionally, they are larger than the average man, are hairy and have beards or other facial hair, engage in rugged activities, and often have leather or rubber fetishes.

A *cub* is someone who is sexually attracted to bears and will often have a similar macho image but are usually younger than the men they are attracted to.

Otters are slimmer and perhaps less hairy bears of any age and *wolves* are usually a more aggressive version of an otter.

131.   What is a *twink*?

A *twink* is a gay man usually in his teens or early twenties who often has a thin body, feminine features, and a preppy image.

132.   What is a *lipstick lesbian?*

A *lipstick lesbian* is a lesbian who is considered very glamorous, fashionable and body conscious.

133.   What is *butch*?

This term describes lesbians who have a masculine or tough image. They usually wear masculine clothing, have short haircuts, and sometimes have tattoos and piercings.

134.   What is *camp*?

Camp refers to someone or something that is theatrical, kitschy, cheesy, exaggerated, effeminate, and dramatic. It can describe members of the gay community who use over-the-top gestures and whose actions and speech are overtly flamboyant.

135.   Why are gay men called *fruits*?

The origin of this term is precisely not clear, but the most likely case is that it comes from the Bible story of Adam and Eve, who were forbidden from eating the fruit in the Garden of Eden. In cultures where gay activity was mostly forbidden, anyone engaging in a homosexual act would be said to be "eating the forbidden fruit".

136. What is a *chicken*?

This refers to a young gay man.

137. Do gay people talk differently from straight people?

Everyone talks in a unique way.

A "Gay Accent" emerged as gay people were becoming more out and proud. It was a camp accent adopted by the more effeminate gay men and made its way into TV and Movie characters during the 90's and naughties.

Because gay people can now be open in mainstream society, there is less need for this type of exaggeration, and camp-speak has more or less faded away, although some die-hard queens still use it.

138. Do gay people walk differently from straight people?

All people, including gay people, walk in a different ways, but for the most part, gay people walk just like everyone else.

Some gay people have adopted a way of walking that is a coded message that tells others they are gay. This is called *mincing* and involves quick, short steps taken with clenched buttocks.

As there is less need for coded flirting now, mincing has more or less died off.

139. Do gay people dress differently from straight people?

Not because they are gay. Everyone has a unique way of dressing.

Some gay people who align themselves to a stereotypical gay image have a flair for drama, theatrics, and outlandish style and usually wear loud and cutting-edge fashion. This may include lots of accessories, revealing clothes, and flashes of brilliant or nightmarish design.

However, most gay people will dress in high-street fashion or business attire, just like everyone else.

140. What is gay bashing?

Some homophobic people verbally attack and physically assault gay people just because they are gay. This is *gay bashing*.

This was once quite common but thankfully less frequent now. That said, some gangs still target gay people, and the police and other groups have done a lot of work to deal with the problem.

Gay people need to be vigilant about the fact that this happens. You may wish to be careful with public displays of affection, particularily late at night, as these attacks are usually carried out by gangs who prowl the streets looking for trouble, so the less you do to attract their attention, the better.

You also need to be mindful of the laws of the country where you live or are visiting. Some countries have very strict rules about public displays of affection, both gay and straight.

Gay people should be able to hold hands and kiss in public where it is acceptable for straight people to do so. However, if you feel like you are in an area that might be intolerant, play it safe so you can avoid being singled out.

If you are assaulted in school as a result of being gay, it is important that you notify the principal or year head to ensure that those who engage in this behaviour are punished and the message goes out in your school that this behaviour is not acceptable.

If you are assaulted on the street, report it to the police. They may connect you to a gay-liaison officer to handle your case.

141. Do gay people live all over the world or just in certain countries?

Studies have shown that gay people live in every corner of the globe, in every country, and in every village, and they are members of every race, tribe, and culture. Every language has words to describe homosexuals.

Particularly conservative political leaders often tell the media that homosexuality doesn't exist in their countries. In such places, reporters have found gay people trying to survive there despite these denials of their existence. Gay people in such countries have to hide their sexuality and live a lie in order to survive.

Many leaders of conservative countries say that homosexuality is an import from Western culture, but words for homosexuality existed in their languages long before they had contact with the West, indicating that they, like every community, have been aware of homosexuality throughout their history. These leaders have chosen to ignore this and to blame the more developed countries for something they do not accept.

As countries become more developed, and the people become more educated, they generally also become more liberal. Eventually, leaders of all countries will see that they have demonised some of their citizens for something that occurs naturally.

In Western society, educated and progressive countries are slowly but surely passing laws granting gay people the equal rights, including the right to get married, to share pensions and tax benefits, to raise families and to inherit property. This has required a long, hard struggle, but that struggle has paid off, and equality will eventually be granted across the globe.

142. How many gay people are there?

Most studies show that between 5 and 10 per cent of all humans are gay, so there are up to 700 million gay people in the world right now.

This also means that if there are 30 people in a class, about 2 or 3 of them are likely to be gay. Being gay crosses all social, racial, religious and ethnic boundaries and people of all colours, ages, and genders are gay.

Many gay people from conservative countries have had to seek refuge in more open countries. Most Western countries will accept gay people as asylum seekers if they come from an area that is intolerant and oppressive to gay people.

143. Do gay people try to make other people gay?

No.

Gay people cannot "turn" someone else, as no one can do anything to influence whether someone is gay or straight.

A gay person may fancy a straight person and wish this other person were also gay, but he or she cannot force a mutual attraction.

144.   Can gay people be parents?

Yes.

Some gay people do not desire to have any children, and they will live happy lives knowing that they will not leave children behind as a legacy. Other gay people do have a desire to be parents and so set about fulfilling this desire.

Some gay people don't ever disclose that they're gay and get married to someone of the opposite sex, have kids, and die without anyone else ever knowing about their true sexual orientation. Others will be out as being gay but make an arrangement with someone of the opposite sex to create a child. They then agree on the best way to protect the welfare of the child and how they will each carry the responsibilities of parenthood. Still others will use the sperm or eggs of donors so that they can fulfil their desire to be parents. Donors may, or may not make further contributions to the rearing of the child.

Gay people who do not want to biologically produce a child can adopt children or become foster parents in most countries.

Some heterosexuals believe that children need both a male and a female figure in their lives, but research shows that a child will develop normally with parents of either gender as long as they know they are loved and are cared for in a secure home. Gay people can provide all that a child needs in abundance.

If you're gay and wish to have a child, consider all the options carefully and decide what is in a child's best interest and not purely in your own.

145.   Do gay parents only have gay children?

No.

Homosexual parents do not necessarily pass homosexuality down through their genes, just as heterosexual parents do not necessarily pass heterosexuality down. That said, some gay parents will have gay children, just as some straight parents have gay children.

If parents are out and open about their sexuality, their children are more likely to feel comfortable about coming out if they are gay. However, children of gay parents are keenly aware that people in their circles are eager to see how they turn out.

Coping with being gay can be a difficult for any child. Children who seem to have all the support they need can still be withdrawn about their sexuality and may need to discuss the situation with someone besides their parents before disclosing their sexual orientation.

Sex is a difficult topic to discuss between any parent and child, and this is no different when the parents are gay.

146.   What can gay people contribute to society?

Gay people are society. They make up 5 to 10 per cent of the population and can be found in any profession, activity, family, and organisation within a society.

Some people believe that gay people are there to support society in ways that heterosexuals may not be able to. In a lot of circumstances, they are childless, which means that they do not always have the same constraints as heterosexuals.

As mentioned elsewhere in the book, gay people are often more available in times of crisis than their straight brothers or sisters to jump into the breach. Let's take a family with four siblings, three of whom are parents and the fourth of whom is gay and childless. Their father has an accident and needs additional care, the gay sibling may be more available to devote his time to the crisis than his straight brothers and sisters because he does not have children to take care of at home.

Gay people are known for their passion and drive in business and some of the most successful business leaders in the world are gay.

Gay people are often quite sensitive, and many gay people take up caring and supporting professions which benefit everyone in society.

Many gay people are also more creative than their heterosexual counterparts and bring tremendous joy to society with their plays, art, writing, movies, comedy, music, sport, and dancing, as the arts and entertainment provide an escape from normal life that everyone needs from time to time.

Gay people are also concerned with the environment, and human rights, and other social issues and often spend their time trying to right the wrongs of the world. Heterosexuals may have the same desire to help out but may be too pre-occupied with their own families to give of their time to the causes they care about.

Gay people are often great thinkers, and some of the greatest philosophers in human history have been gay. They have been responsible for great inventions and scientific breakthroughs because they were able to dedicate more time to their work than other people.

147. Can gay couples get married?

In most Western countries, gay couples can legally marry or register a civil union. This gives them the same rights as those afforded to heterosexual married couples, including tax breaks and pension and inheritance rights. Some choose to marry in a ceremony attended by their friends and family, just as heterosexuals do. Some anomalies still exist in the laws, but the gay rights movement continues to work for full equality.

That said, a lot of religions do not condone same-sex unions, and homosexual couples may not be able to have their marriage ceremonies in a house of prayer or have their unions blessed by a member of the clergy. In time, even religious leaders will have to face the fact that members of their faiths are gay and should be afforded the same respect, rights, and privileges as heterosexual members.

148.   What is a civil union?

A civil union is the legal recognition of two people as a couple. Gay people can now declare their relationship to be a legally binding union in most Western countries.

Depending on the locality, a civil union offers all or most of the entitlements of marriage.

149.   What is LGBT?

This is the collective term for everyone in the gay community. It stands for *lesbian*, *gay*, *bisexual*, and *transgender* – all of which are explained in this book.

150.   Do gay men really just want to be girls, and do lesbians really just want to be boys?

No.

Most gay men want to be men, and they just happen to be attracted to other men. Sometimes gay men display more traits that are considered feminine than their heterosexual peers, but they are still men in mind and body.

Likewise, lesbians are women whose female identities are important to them, and they just happen to be attracted to other women.

151.   Why does the media tend to portray all lesbians in a masculine manner?

Lesbians have often been portrayed very unfairly in mainstream media as tough and aggressive women.

Thankfully that image is slowly changing. In recent times there have been some very positive moves in TV and Movies to show the more glamorous side to gay women, and that they can be found in every facet of life and throughout every part of the world and of every race, colour and creed.

Naturally, there are some very strong personalities among the lesbian community, just as there are softer and very gentle personalities.

152.   Are gay relationships monogamous?

Usually.

Some couples will decide to remain monogamous (sexual and romantic only with each other) and sexual activity with anyone else is not allowed. Some couples will agree to allow sex outside the relationship but within specific boundaries, while others will agree to be faithful to each other emotionally but allow each other to have sex with whomever they wish.

Each couple decides what is right for them. As with any relationship, each person must operate within the boundaries or trust will break down and the relationship will falter.

153.   Is everyone who in a traditional marriage (one between opposite genders) straight?

No.

Some people marry partners of the opposite gender to avoid having to deal with being gay. They'll live as straight people and go through the motions of married life. Sometimes this works out and they can live contented lives, but a part of them will always be curious about what their life would have been like if they had been true to themselves, and they never discover what a fully authentic existence is like.

Others inform their opposite-sex partner that they are gay and agree for the sake of a business, family, or child that it is best to pretend to the world that they are both straight. Such couples usually manage to drift along successfully under these circumstances.

In generations past, people did not always have the opportunity to be themselves because society did not understand or tolerate gay people, so many gay people found themselves entering conventional marriages just to fit in with mainstream society.

Many gay people remain secretly trapped in such marriages throughout their lives, but in other situations, they come clean to their spouses about their sexuality. This can be a really difficult situation and their spouse often finds it difficult to recover from the deception. Both parties in this case need as much support as they can get to navigate this disclosure and to decide how to proceed. Therapists can often be the best source of support in this situation.

Children can usually get to a place of understanding when they discover that one of their parents is gay, once they've had time to adjust to the idea. They do need reassurances that they were wanted by both parents, and that they are still loved by both parents.

The family members will need some time and space while trying to deal with the disclosure, and positive outcomes are possible if everyone tries to be respectful and understanding.

Some married men who are gay may seek out sex from other men by cruising seedy parks or public toilets, or they pay a male prostitute to fulfil their natural sexual urges. If these sexual partners do not practice safe sex, the men involved risk contracting sexually transmitted diseases and, in turn, transmitting them to their wives.

They also run the risk of being caught and outed, which means they can't control how and when their families find out that they're gay. This can lead to a nightmarish situation because the revelation of the deception leads to the breakdown of trust.

If you're living a lie, remember that you have one life to live. Your circumstances will dictate whether you feel comfortable informing your family about your true sexual orientation, but in any case, you need to be careful about the activities you engage in and consider the consequences of any actions you partake in.

Most gay communities have support groups for gay people who are leading straight lives, joining such a group could be useful for you. *See resource section.*

154. What is gay curious?

People do not know what a sexual urge is until they have one, so adolescents often mistake an infatuation with a peer as love or a sexual attraction. Many boys and girls play a "show me yours and I'll show you mine" game, and in some cases this casual sexual activity can cause arousal. If this happens between members of the same gender, this does not necessarily mean they are gay.

As an adolescent, it is normal to get aroused by anything to do with sex, and adolescents are curious about sex, and this is perfectly normal.

If a sexual urge for people of your own gender remains and you masturbate to images or sexual thoughts about sexual activity between people of your own gender, then you may be gay. During your teens, you'll discover patterns in what arouses you sexually, and if one of these is that people of your own gender arouse you, then you probably are gay.

There is no hurry to figure it all out. It will naturally occur to you whether you are gay or straight or bisexual or asexual.

Enjoy your curious years, and don't be alarmed by any urges or desires you have. Whatever it is, it is natural, so whatever you think and feel is part of normal human nature. Remember, however, that children are never to be involved in any of your sexual experimentation. Ensure that all parties fully consent to any exploration.

155.   I am in my elder years and have never come out. Should I bother now?

You have one life to live, and it's your choice how to live it.

Don't be hard on yourself, as you grew up in a time when coming out just wasn't an easy option. You may have entered into a traditional marriage and even had kids and maybe even have grandkids now. Or you may have lived as a single person and just lived a lie for all these years, pretending that the right person for marriage never came along.

Whatever the case, it is good that you're being honest with yourself and accepting your sexuality now. You know best whether changing the status quo is beneficial for you at this point.

You may wish to join a support group for people in a similar situation by contacting the gay helpline in your area to discuss the matter. You'll likely find comfort in meeting other people in the same situation as yourself, and these people may be able to assist you and give you advice because they've dealt with coming out in later years. *See resource section.*

156. Are prisoners gay if they have sex with each other?

Not necessarily. Some prisoners are gay and would be so inside or outside of prison. Other prisoners are heterosexual but may have sexual relations in prison with someone of their gender as a means of releasing sexual frustration.

When they get out of prison, these people usually and organically revert to their original heterosexual identities.

157.   What is multiple oppression?

Multiple oppression occurs when one person is a part of more than one minority group whose members are oppressed within his or her society. For example, you could be both gay and disabled, or gay and a member of an ethnic minority.

Any combination of minority identities adds complexity to a person's life, and people with multiple minority identities often need more support to get through their various challenges.

158.   Why are gay people bullied?

Interestingly, gay people tend to be bullied more when they're in the closet, as once they've come out, they take control, and so take power away from the bullies.

This time between realisation that you're gay and coming out is the worst. Gay people may even bully other gay people in a desperate attempt to hide their true identities.

Bullies may pick up on elements of the personalities of gay people that make them different and tease or torture them because of it. It is widely known that gay people are more likely to be bullied in school than other students, and gay and lesbian organisations in Western culture are working to combat this.

If you're gay and being bullied in school, talk with the school counsellor or a trusted teacher. They'll likely work to address the situation, but if nothing gets done, talk with your principal or head so he or she enacts the school's anti-bullying policy.

Remember, bullying usually eases or even disappears when you accept yourself, as they have no weapons to use against you.

159. Should I tell my employer that I'm gay?

In most cases, being gay is all right in the workplace and is protected by anti-discrimination laws that ensure you get fair treatment in the workplace.

There is no onus on you to declare your sexual orientation to your employers or work colleagues, but at the same time, there is no onus on you to hide the fact that you're gay.

Your employer may have made comments about gay people that you find offensive or have otherwise indicated that he or she is homophobic. This may mean that you have less chance of promotion than your straight colleagues. If you feel you've been passed over for promotion because you're gay, you can challenge your employer's decisions on grounds of discrimination. You don't have to accept this treatment, and you may want to make your views known to your firm's human resources department. It is important that gay people in the workplace stand up for their rights to ensure fairness for everyone.

160. Could my career be affected if people at work know that I am gay?

In almost every Westernised society, employment law gives people the right to be exempt from discrimination in the workplace. It is important to keep a note of times and dates of comments and discussions about your sexuality in the workplace and their context and outcomes. You may never need this information, but it will help you if you ever need to take action against your colleagues or employers if you feel undermined because you are gay.

Most colleagues and employers will be supportive, and your sexuality won't matter to them. However, in more aggressive environments, your sexuality may make you the subject of teasing. You may take a light-hearted approach to general teasing if it's done with the right attitude; however, if you feel you're being undermined or prevented from progressing within the company because of your sexuality, you may need to bring up the teasing with human resources, your boss, or a lawyer.

161.   Can I be fired for being gay?

Not in most situations.

Most Western countries have anti-discrimination laws which ensure that gay people (and members of other minority groups) cannot be discriminated against in the workplace. If you were fired or let go and you think this happened only because of your sexuality, you should contact your equality authority or a legal advisor.

In some western countries, loopholes may exist in the laws when it comes to employees of religious organisations. In an institution such as a Catholic school, they may be able to dismiss you if they discover that you do not adhere to their religious dogma in your private life. If you work for such an institution, you might feel that it's best to wait until the laws are changed before you disclose that you're gay. You may also wish to participate in the process of getting those laws changed.

162.   Are gay people discriminated against in other parts of society?

Sometimes, but less so now than in the past.

Some people have been conditioned by their families, religious groups, or cultures to see gayness as something unusual, not to be encouraged, and even wrong, so they discriminate against people who are gay.

Most liberal countries have laws protecting gay people from discrimination. This would include areas like memberships to clubs, entry to venues, protection from hate crimes, redress for slander, rights to services and medical care, rights to participate in politics and rights to all other elements of society just as everyone else has.

If you feel that you are being discriminated against, you likely have options for legal redress. Consult your local gay support service or speak to a lawyer.

Gay people should not feel discriminated against. Being gay is not a choice and so should not affect your treatment in society.

163. Can homosexuality be cured?

There is no medical problem with being gay, so it not something to be cured or treated. It is a fact of life, so it needs to be accepted.

164. Should gay people have therapy?

Not necessarily.

Most gay people will pass through adolescence and into adulthood needing no more than self-acceptance and the support of family and friends. However, many gay students find support from a school counsellor or a trusted teacher to be helpful, as these people can give the students safe outlets for their feelings when times are tough.

Adult gay people may also need support, and counsellors and therapists can offer a safe and understanding environment for these people to talk through their experiences of growing up with a secret and can help them work through any problems they have.

165. Are there a lot of drugs in the gay scene?

The gay scene, like any club scene, is permeated by drugs.

Gay people who have had a difficult time accepting themselves sometimes reach for something that will allow them to escape the pressures of life, and these include nicotine, alcohol, and other drugs.

If you get into the gay scene, you will inevitably be offered drugs, and it's important that you make the correct choices – as all people have to do.

In school, you will have been given all the warnings about what drugs can do to your body and your mind, and you need to think carefully about this information as you make your choices. Most people who decide to take drugs will lead more dysfunctional lives and develop health problems earlier than others, as the human body does not deal with these substances easily. Addiction sets in very easily, quickly making the problems that you attempted to escape become secondary to problems that arise from your addiction.

166. Why is the term *gay* used in a negative way as slang?

Teenagers have been using the word *gay* to describe something that is lame, silly, or stupid. It is not clear how this caught on, as it did so just as society was really getting a handle on the fact that being gay is okay.

It is offensive. Its origin lies in homophobic attitudes from the 1970s and '80s, and teenagers adopted it after hearing their parents' use it to describe their attitudes to homosexuality.

If you hear the term used in a negative way, ask the user how they would feel if they were gay and heard it. That person will say that you can't take a joke or that no harm was meant, but if you speak up, people will realise that it's offensive.

The term's use will pass, just as all slang dies out, but there will probably always be homophobic people and bigots within society.

167. Why do gay people get killed or jailed in some countries?

Cultures in some parts of the world have yet to accept that gay people have no choice about their sexuality and punish anyone who takes part in a homosexual act.

These places usually have legal systems that are intertwined with religion (a theocracy), and if the state religion holds that homosexuality is wrong, then that will become encoded in the law. Many people who live in such countries cannot separate their religious beliefs from their home lives, school lives, work lives, social lives, or political lives.

Unfortunately, these ancient religious teachings sometimes require that gay people be punished for being born gay, and in the worst cases, gay people have been beaten, jailed, and even executed.

In time, as people in less developed countries become better educated, they too will see that their gay citizens are equal to everyone else and they will change the laws to reflect this, however, it will probably be a slow process.

168. What is the rainbow flag?

The rainbow flag (a flag of many colours) was carried during pride marches in the United States in the 1970s and has since become a symbol for the LGBT community. The colours symbolise diversity and show that gay people are part of the diversity of nature. The LGBT rainbow flag should always be displayed with the red stripe on top or to the left to distinguish it from other rainbow flags.

Some gay people like to link the rainbow flag to the song "Somewhere Over the Rainbow" from *The Wizard of Oz*, as this is an iconic movie in gay society.

169. Are all gay men effeminate?

No.

Some gay men are effeminate, and some straight men are effeminate. Today, most gay people do not need to accentuate their personalities and simply act like everyone else. Those people who are effeminate by nature are entitled to be themselves, just as everyone else is, and they should not have to face ridicule or taunting just for being themselves.

170. Did gay people cause AIDS?

No.

No one knows exactly where AIDS originated, but it is widely accepted that it first occurred in the 1930s and first entered the human population in the late 1950s. Most theories point towards its origins being within primates in Africa, who somehow then transmitted the virus to humans. Some people have said that this happened because humans had sexual intercourse with chimpanzees; however, it may have been transmitted during the hunting of chimpanzees, when their blood got into human hunters' open cuts. It may also have originated in medical experiments in Africa in the 1950s, when samples of treated chimp tissue were inserted into humans in the hope of finding a cure for polio. For most of us, it is not important where it began, but it is important for all people to know how to prevent getting it.

Gay men have a high risk of contracting HIV if they do not use condoms, as the virus is easily transmitted through anal sex.

The HIV virus has been the subject of a lot of medical research, and people who have it now have a better chance of living relatively normal lives than they did in the past with advancements in medical treatment. If HIV is not treated and it takes hold, it can lead to AIDS, which is a more difficult disease to manage.

One rule of thumb for everyone is that when it comes to having sex, treat everyone as if they could be a carrier of the virus and use a condom for every act of sex, avoid swallowing semen, and avoid mixing your bodily fluids with others'.

For more information, see the next section, "Questions about Gay Sex and Sexual Health".

171. What is gaydar?

Gaydar is a play on the word *radar*, and it refers to the ability to try and guess whether other people in the vicinity are gay. The term was most commonly used by gay people when they would try to identify other gay people in mixed company before homosexuality was widely accepted.

People would use their gaydar to pick up on body language, phrases, tone of voice, and mannerisms that might indicate whether someone was gay and then make subtle gestures to test if they were interested or wanted to meet somewhere more private. Gaydar is now also the name of a popular social media space where gay people connect with each other online.

172. Is gay life isolating?

Not if you don't want it to be.

Some people like a solitary life, and others like to be surrounded by people all the time. Everyone is different.

In times past, being gay was difficult, as many people kept their orientation to themselves. Gay people might be surrounded by family and friends and sometimes got married and had kids, but they couldn't allow other people to know about their innermost feelings about their attraction to people of their own gender. This fact of life was isolating, as people did not feel as if they would be accepted in society if others knew that they were gay.

Now, gay people are found in every part of society and are plumbers and politicians, stay-at-home moms and pop stars. No longer do people whisper in corners about someone who is gay, although a small portion of society still discriminates against gay people.

Finding a partner can still be challenging, and gay people in search of partners can feel lonely, but no more that straight people in the same situation.

It is important for gay people, as it is for everyone, to maintain good friendships, family bonds, and working relations and to be active members of their societies. Doing so will ensure a strong network of supporters in times of need and a strong network of partygoers in good times.

173. What is a gay icon?

Throughout the history of the gay movement, some people have been hailed as icons.

These icons have been people at the forefront of campaigns for equality, film stars who were particularly glamorous, pop stars who were supporters of the gay rights movement, gay people who happened to be famous, and even cartoon and movie characters.

Every movement needs heroes. Those in the gay movement often like to have glamorous heroes.

174. Why do gay people love musicals?

Not all gay people love musicals, but musicals have always been associated with the gay movement.

One theory is that musicals offer glamour, fantasy, escapism, style, finesse, mystery, humour, and the type of theatrics that some participants in the gay rights movement adopt themselves, as gay people often had to over-emphasise their flamboyancy in order to show the world that they were out and proud.

More recently, the movement has lost some of the pageantry and flamboyancy that it once had, but perhaps that's progress!

175. What is a diva?

A diva is someone whose ego is over the top. Divas are usually very demanding, bitchy, self-centred, dramatic, provocative, and often amusing.

The gay community tends to contain a large population of divas. This may have something to do with the fact that in the past, gay people needed to be overly persuasive to be accepted, and some people like to push boundaries.

Eccentrics are among the gay community, as they are among every community, and they contribute to the colourful, diverse mix of people who make up the grand tapestry of life.

176. Why is pink traditionally associated with gay people?

During the Second World War, the Nazis decided that gay people were to be eradicated and forced anyone suspected of being gay to wear a pink triangle.

The colour pink and the pink triangle has been used since in defiance of this horrendous homophobia.

177. Is the word *queer* offensive?

People used to use the term *queer* to refer negatively to gay people, and it is sometimes still used in that way. However, the gay community has reclaimed it and now often use it in a friendly way to defy the prejudice that it once conveyed.

178. Are only humans gay?

No.

Homosexual activity has been observed in more than 1,500 species of animals, with humans being just one of those species.

Examples of homosexual activity have been observed in dolphins, bison, gulls, dogs, vultures, monkeys (and most other primates), elephants, ducks, giraffes, gut worms, lions, cats, sheep, hyenas, fruit flies, swans, lizards, pigeons, and penguins.

Through scientific observation, we can see that homosexuality is in a being's nature, irrespective of its nurturing. Non-human animals act on their natural instincts, so gay humans should be free to act on their instincts within the same boundaries as heterosexual humans do – without prejudice.

179. Is support available for gay people?

Absolutely.

Most gay communities offer online and live support groups for gay people coming out, older people, married people, parents, lesbians, alcoholics, the unemployed, those who are depressed and many other groupings within the gay community. There are many books, leaflets, sports and other special-interest groups, dating events, holidays, and so on to support gay people.

If no "in-person" support groups exist in your area, look online for the nearest support centre in your country and visit if you can. You may need to try a few groups to see where you feel most comfortably within the gay community.

Your area probably also has a gay helpline that can be found through an online search. This line can let you know what types of resources are available in your area, will listen to your story, and will help you to cope with your stage of acceptance.

You can also speak with a counsellor in your school, college, or community. Such professionals are often also great resources for more information.

See resource section at the back of this book to find a link that could lead to your local support services.

Questions about Gay Sex and Sexual Health

180. How does gay sex work?

Gay people are romantic souls just like everyone else. When gay people get together, they usually engage in courtship and flirting first. As with straight couples, initial gestures such as hugging, touching, stroking, kissing, rubbing, and fondling begin romantic adventures. When gay people decide it is time to become more physical, they will usually engage in more intimate activities such as foreplay and then perhaps move on to oral stimulation before they attempt any penetrative activity.

For gay men, the act of sexual intercourse usually requires one partner to be active (a *top*) and the other partner to be passive (a *bottom*), and the basic act of sexual activity involves the top's penis penetrating the bottom's bottom – usually with the help of some lubrication and preferably with a condom. The general result is that both parties reach orgasm and ejaculate.

Some people are only tops, some only bottoms, and some, referred to as *versatile*, can be either. It depends on their preference.

When both parties are tops, they usually do everything except anal penetration to reach climax. When both parties are bottoms, they also usually do similar activities, but one may take the role of a top.

For lesbians, sex can involve any form of sexual stimulation that satisfies each partner. This usually involves stimulation of the vagina and other erogenous zones for each person. Lesbians can reach orgasm through use of tongues, fingers, vibrators, or other sex toys.

181. Does anal sex make you sore?

Anal sex is like all sex – it involves muscles. When you exercise any muscle for the first time, it takes time to adjust to this new movement. This activity may leave you sore at first, but as the muscles adapt to new movements, they become accustomed to these activities and eventually relax.

182. What is oral sex?

This involves using your mouth, tongue, breath, and lips to stimulate the sexual organs of your partner. It involves licking and sucking mostly, but it can involve flicking, blowing, massaging, and nibbling – although it's best not to use your teeth too forcefully in the course of your work.

183. What is gay porn?

Pornography (porn) is the explicit portrayal of sexual activity in text, photographs, animation, sound recordings, film, video, and video games designed to titillate the observer.

It can be bought or sourced in newsagents, adult stores, and sex clubs, although the vast majority of porn is now sourced online.

Gay porn is porn whose subject matter pertains to gay sexual activities.

184.   What is a gay sauna or bathhouse?

A gay sauna or bathhouse is a place where gay adults (mostly men) go for casual sex in a safe environment. It is usually a place with saunas, jacuzzis, steam rooms, and showers where only towels are worn.

If people at a sauna or bathhouse are attracted to each other, they can have a sexual encounter in private areas within the facility. These venues are found in most large cities in the developed world.

185.   What is a gay fetish?

As heterosexuals do, gay people can have fetishes, which are fantasy aspects of their sexuality. Some people prefer to have sex that involves sex toys, leather, rubber, pain, whips, and other accessories.

As long as all parties know and consent to the activity and will not be harmed by it, then to each their own.

186.   What is a rent boy?

A *rent boy* is a young male prostitute. Many boys who end up in this business have been rejected by their families and moved away to a big city. Soon the costs of living in a city bear down on them, and they revert to selling their bodies for sex to pay the bills.

The life of a rent boy can be very sad and dangerous, and it often involves drugs and violence. Prostitutes are prone to becoming HIV positive if they're not careful about protection or if they are raped.

Sometimes people just choose to use their bodies to make a living and do not have the other baggage that I mentioned. Not all rent boys live in cities, either. They can be found in smaller communities, but it is harder to keep anonymous among a smaller population.

187.   What is cottaging?

Cottaging happens when gay men meet in public places such as public toilets or public parks to engage in anonymous sexual activity. There is an element of danger involved, and this can be part of the attraction. However, this practice is carried out mostly by people who are married or in other relationships in which they must keep their sexual identities secret and who want to have a sexual release without any relationship ties.

188.   What is cruising?

Cruising is the act of gay people checking each other out. It usually happens in public, but it can also happen in nightclubs or bars. Cruising is usually about hooking up with someone just for sex without a relationship.

189.   What are poppers?

Poppers have been part of the gay scene since the 1970s. It is the inhalation of vapours of alkyl nitrates (and other nitrates) to enhance sexual pleasure. The vapours assist in relaxing the muscles, which allows for easier penetration during sex.

There is mixed information on the damage poppers can do, but it is widely accepted that they can cause damage to your brain, respiratory and cardiovascular systems, and vision if used extensively.

Tread carefully!

190.   Are a lot of gay people also paedophiles?

No.

Paedophiles exist in every society, and some gay people also happen to be paedophiles.

There is the same proportion of paedophiles among gay people as there are among straight people, so the vast majority of paedophiles are straight.

Whether gay or straight, it is imperative that people who are sexually attracted to children speak to their doctors about these desires *before ever acting on them*. Their doctors will put them in touch with specialist therapists to help them to deal with these urges and keep from harming any child.

191. Are gay people more promiscuous than straight people?

This depends on your definition of promiscuity.

Gay people and straight people think about sex around the same amount, but gay people tend to act on these thoughts more than straight people so the truth is that in general, gay people are more promiscuous than straight people.

Lesbian women tend to be less promiscuous than gay men, however they have a higher rate of promiscuity than their straight female counterparts. Lesbian women are also more likely to have sex with a man during their lifetime than a gay man is to have sex with a woman.

Gay Males tend to be somewhat more promiscuous than their straight counterparts – probably in defiance of the constraints of conventional living. Males who are not romantically connected to each other can view sex as purely a physical encounter and can have sex without the emotional ties.

Gay couples sometimes have a more liberal view of relationships needing to be monogamous. Some people in gay relationships can have sexual contact outside the union without this negatively impacting the relationship – so long as agreed boundaries are adhered to. There is a different dynamic between two people of the same gender than between two people of opposite genders.

192. Do straight people have sex with members of their own gender?

Not usually.

Straight people are largely only sexually attracted to people of the opposite gender. However, some straight people will have sex with someone of their own gender as an experiment, perhaps to make sure they're straight and not bisexual or gay. They usually don't find it as stimulating or exciting as sex with someone of the opposite gender.

In extreme situations (as mentioned earlier) such as in prison, straight people will sometimes have sex with someone of the same gender in order to relieve sexual tension. This does not alter their sexual orientation and they return to heterosexual activity when they are back in their normal environment.

193. What is an open relationship?

Some couples decide that they want to have an open relationship, which means although they are emotionally committed to each other, they are each allowed to have sexual encounters with others outside the relationship.

This arrangement can be dangerous if the boundaries are not clearly defined, but it can be managed when everyone is honest and open about their behaviour and feelings.

194. Do gay relationships last?

Some do and some don't – like all relationships.

As time goes on, more and more long-term gay relationships are holding up because people can live their lives openly without the stress of having to keep their private lives a secret.

Gay people have the same desire to avoid loneliness in later life and to share their lives with a partner. They usually do not have the glue of children to keep their relationships going, so gay people may have to work harder than others to keep their relationships fresh and interesting to ensure it endures.

As more and more countries legalise civil unions, gay people are now offered the same opportunity to publicly declare their love for each other as straight people, and the legal aspect of this union can help to cement these relationships. As with all relationships, some last, and some don't.

195.   Is being gay all about sex?

No.

Being gay is only one aspect of your personality, but it does reach into almost every aspect of life.

There are so many facets to your life, including sexuality, but you have so much to do, see, experience, and deal with that has nothing to do with sex.

Live your life to the full, and don't define your life only by your sexuality. Embrace it and enjoy being gay, but don't let it control everything you do.

196.   Why can gay men not donate blood in some countries?

Some countries have banned blood donations from all men who have had anal sex with other men. Technically, gay men can donate blood if they haven't engaged in this activity.

The blood transfusion services in these places take a view that actively gay men are at a higher risk for HIV, so blood donations from them carry a higher risk of being HIV positive.

This is a contentious issue within the gay community. Most gay people are responsible about their sexual activities and regularly get checked for STI's. They believe that their blood poses no greater risk than anyone else's and that the medical authorities are turning their backs on millions of badly needed healthy blood donations every year.

This ban is likely to be overturned in the near future.

197. What is HIV?

HIV stands for human immunodeficiency virus. This is a virus that attacks your immune system, leaving it unable to fight infections and cancers or heal other sicknesses and injuries. When you contract the disease, you are *HIV positive*.

HIV is passed from one person to another through bodily fluids, including blood, semen, breast milk, and vaginal fluids, and people are infected when the virus enters their bloodstreams.

If HIV goes untreated, it can cause acquired immunodeficiency syndrome, or AIDS, which is more difficult to treat and live with. However, anti-retroviral therapies have greatly reduced the incidence of progression from HIV to AIDS and have allowed many people to live full lives.

Most gay people who are HIV positive contracted the disease through an exchange of semen, blood, or both. The best way to avoid contracting HIV is to treat all sexual partners as if they were HIV positive. Always use condoms when engaging in sexual activity, particularly with someone whose status you do not know.

198. How do you become HIV positive?

The most common method that gay people contract the HIV virus is through anal sex and the exchange of fluids during the process. As anal sex does not provide the same natural lubrication as vaginal sex, it can cause bleeding in the anus where the semen is released. If the fluids of someone who is HIV positive get into the bloodstream of someone who is HIV negative, there is a strong chance that the virus will infect the negative person.

People who inject drugs such as heroin can also pass the infection to each other by sharing infected needles. Another method of contracting HIV is through blood transfusions, but all donated blood is currently screened to reduce the risk of this happening. Mothers can also pass on HIV to their unborn children during pregnancy or birth, and to their babies through breastfeeding.

However, you won't get HIV from hugging, touching, shaking hands, or kissing. You cannot get it from toilet seats, swimming pools, drinking from other people's cups, using their phones, or other casual contact, as HIV does not survive outside the body for very long.

199. How do I avoid HIV and AIDS?

You need to be cautious, and keep yourself informed yourself about the dangers of HIV, AIDS, and other sexually transmitted diseases and infections.

To give yourself the best chance for remaining HIV negative, treat everyone as if they are HIV positive until you know their status for sure. Wear a condom for intercourse and for oral sex. If you are at a substantial risk of becoming HIV positive (e.g. if you are a sex worker or you are in a relationship with someone who is HIV positive or you share heroin needles) you might consider taking a drug called Pre-Exposure Prophylaxis (PrEP). If you are not on PrEP and you ever feel like you have been exposed to the HIV virus, you should go to your doctor and obtain a drug called Post-Exposure Prophylaxis (PEP). You must take this within 72 hours of the exposure to try and prevent you from contracting the virus.

HIV and AIDS are a risk to everyone, not just gay people. In fact, in global terms, straight women are at most risk for contracting HIV and currently have the highest incidence of HIV, so using a condom during casual heterosexual casual sex is strongly advised also.

There is no 100 per cent foolproof way to avoid contracting the disease, so be careful.

200. Why are gay people associated with HIV and AIDS?

When AIDS became an epidemic in the 1980s, it was called the "gay curse", as people saw it as a disease specific to gay men. At the time, the use of condoms was not widespread, and people were unaware of the dangers of swapping bodily fluids internally. This was true for gay and straight people, and all kinds of diseases were being passed between partners.

Unfortunately, while the media was busy highlighting the fact that AIDS affected gay people, straight people were passing it along unwittingly, and even today there are tens of millions more people being infected annually, because of unprotected sex.

HIV and AIDS are not gay diseases. They are sexually transmitted diseases.

201. If I become HIV positive, will I die?

Probably not. In fact, you're more likely to live a relatively healthy, normal life than you would have in the past now that antiretroviral drugs can generally stabilise your condition.

If HIV progresses to AIDS, the condition is more difficult to treat. This progression can take approximately eight years, and if it does, the immune system has more difficulty fighting infections.

Get regular check-ups, including blood screenings, to check for HIV so you can get the disease diagnosed at an early stage if you do happen to contract it. Doing so will greatly improve your chances of remaining healthy.

202. I think I may be HIV positive or have AIDS. What do I do?

Go to your GP or go to a sexual health clinic immediately. Ask for a full sexually transmitted infection (STI) screening, and then await the results. Whatever the outcome, you'll receive appropriate treatment.

Stigma and shame prevented people in the past from getting the appropriate tests if they thought they might be infected. Many people (including celebrities) are now challenging the stigma of HIV and AIDS and eliminating any shame associated with having the condition.

203. What other sexually transmitted infections (STIs) should I be aware of?

Apart from HIV and AIDS, there are around thirty other sexually transmitted infections to watch out for. The following are the most common within the gay community.

Chlamydia: This is a bacterial infection that usually found in the urethra. Antibiotics are an effective treatment.

Genital warts (human papillomavirus, or HPV): Sores or lumps on the genitals. Treatable by the STI clinic or your doctor. Vaccinations are now available for some forms of this virus so that it can be prevented entirely in the future.

Genital herpes: Lesions or sores on the body, sometimes accompanied by flu-like symptoms. There is no known cure, but treatments are getting better all the time.

Hepatitis: A disease of the liver that comes in five general forms – A, B, C, D, and E. Each has a different treatment, but the best way to avoid any of them is to get immunised against them. You can get the jabs from your doctor or an STI clinic.

Syphilis: This often starts with a sore on the mouth and is caught from kissing or having oral sex with an infected person. Antibiotics usually clear it up, but it must be caught early. Have regular check-ups to ensure you do.

Gonorrhoea: This is often caught from oral sex also, and it first manifests as a sore throat. Antibiotics can clear it up if it's caught early.

Crabs (pubic lice): These are insect parasites passed from person to person, usually through close physical contact. This is easily treated with a special shampoo from the pharmacy. However, if it's not caught early while it is still confined to the pubic area, it can spread to the hair on your head and even eyebrows.

Trichomonas vaginalis (TV, trich): This is a vaginal protozoan infection that can be passed between lesbians who share sex toys. It is treatable with medication.

Non-specific urethritis (NSU): A bacterial infection of the penis that causes discomfort and pain, particularly during urination. This can be treated with antibiotics if it's caught early.

If you suspect that you have an STI, then abstain from sex until you've had it treated to prevent passing it on. It is easy to pick up infections, and the more sexual partners you have, the greater your chances for picking one up.

As you can see, most of these are treatable, but you must have regular check-ups to remain as safe as possible and to catch anything you pick up at an early stage. Most large cities have free STI screening clinics for gay people. *See resource section.*

204. Okay, now that I know all about gay life and I fully accept myself as being gay, how do I find a partner?

Straight people face the same challenges that you do, except you have the added challenge of a smaller pool of people to choose from.

People find partners anywhere, from chance meetings in their neighbourhood to trips across the globe to seek them out.

Attending gay specific festivals, events, venues, groups, campaigns, sports clubs or support groups will at least put you among a population of people who are also going to be gay.

If you don't find someone through real life activities, you could try online dating, perhaps on one of the many social media outlets dedicated to gay dating. Many gay dating smartphone apps. with GPS location allow you to see other app. users in your neighbourhood and beyond. Proximity can be important, as many people find long-distance relationships difficult. *Grindr* is a popular gay app. for casual encounters while relationships are often found through a site like *Gaydar* (all dating apps are only suitable for people of aged eighteen and over).

You are more likely to make a good match with someone as physically as attractive as you, as financially secure as you, as clever as you, and with similar morals and values as you. However, the most unlikely couples can make it against the odds, so give people a fair chance if they show a healthy interest.

If a relationship doesn't work out, it is pointless to beat yourself up about it and wonder what went wrong. You just weren't suited to each other, and there isn't anything wrong with you. Keep trying, and don't take dating too seriously. When you find yourself between relationships, single life can also be fun.

Enjoy your gay life, make it as fun, fulfilling, purposeful, and healthy as you can.

Good luck!

Online Resources

International

List of LGBT Rights Organisations throughout the world: http://en.wikipedia.org/wiki/List_of_LGBT_rights_organizations

Parents/Family /Friends of Lesbians and Gays – http://www.pflag.org

International Lesbian and Gay Human Rights Commission - https://iglhrc.org/

Global LGBT Online Campaigns - https://www.allout.org/en

U.S.A

National GLBT National Help Centre -http://www.glbtnationalhelpcenter.org/

National Association of LGBT Community Centers www.lgbtcenters.org

Canada

Central Toronto Youth Services - http://www.ctys.org/category/groups/

LGBT Youth Helpline - http://www.youthline.ca/

UK

Helplines Partnership – Go to this website and click the LGBT Section for the latest listing of Local LGBT Helplines in the UK - http://search.helplines.org/

National Consortium of LGBT Organisations and Supports

http://www.lgbtconsortium.org.uk/directory

Ireland

National LGBT Helpline – 1890929539 - http://www.lgbt.ie/

Australia

National LGBTI Health Alliance – List of LGBT organisations http://www.lgbthealth.org.au/

National Helpline Listings - http://www.helplines.org.au/

LGBT Helpline - Gay and Lesbian Helpline: 03 9663 2939

New Zealand

Gay NZ – Listing of National and local services and events - http://www.gaynz.com/community/

NZ Gay Switchboard - (04) 473 7878

Africa

International Gay and Lesbian Human Rights Commission - Africa

http://iglhrc.org/region/africa

Asia

List of resources and activities for LGBT people in Asia

http://www.utopia-asia.com/

Latin America and Caribbean

International Gay and Lesbian Human Rights Commission - Latin America and Caribbean

http://iglhrc.org/region/latin-america-and-caribbean

Russia

Russian LGBT Network

http://www.lgbtnet.ru

Middle East

Informal website with some useful links to resources and LGBT groups

Queer Jihad - http://www.well.com/user/queerjhd/

Further Questions for Future Editions

If you have other questions about how to deal with being gay or about supporting someone else who is gay just email the author at - completegayguide@gmail.com

He will try to answer your question personally by email. Your question and his answer may be included in future editions of the book (Your identity will not be disclosed unless you wish to be acknowledged for your input).

About the Author

Michael Ryan was born in Ireland.

He is a counsellor and psychotherapist in Dublin, Ireland. He works with children and teenagers in schools and with adults in his private practice.

He is an active member of the gay community and the LGBT movement. He came out as being gay to his family and friends when he was twenty-seven years old.

He is also a human rights activist and volunteers with national and international charities and community groups at the board and grassroots levels.

He has been involved in radio shows on human rights issues as a producer, researcher, and presenter and regularly features in mainstream media to comment on LGBT and human rights issues.

He wrote The Complete Guide to Gay Life for New Explorers to help gay people come to terms with their sexuality early in their discovery process to perhaps save them from some of the pain and isolation he felt while he needlessly carried around his secret.

He has been with his partner, Gavin, since 1998.

Lightning Source UK Ltd.
Milton Keynes UK
UKOW04f0707060115

244048UK00002B/157/P